Changing Gender Relations, Changing Families

) (

THE GENDER LENS SERIES

Series Editors

Judith A. Howard
University of Washington

Barbara Risman
University of Illinois, Chicago

Joey Sprague
University of Kansas

The Gender Lens series has been conceptualized as a way of encouraging the development of a sociological understanding of gender. A "gender lens" means working to make gender visible in social phenomena; asking if, how, and why social processes, standards, and opportunities differ systematically for women and men. It also means recognizing that gender inequality is inextricably braided with other systems of inequality. The Gender Lens series is committed to social change directed toward eradicating these inequalities. Originally published by Sage Publications and Pine Forge Press, all Gender Lens books are now available from The Rowman & Littlefield Publishing Group.

BOOKS IN THE SERIES

Changing Gender Relations, Changing Families

Tracing the Pace of Change over Time

Oriel Sullivan

) (

Rowman & Littlefield Publishers, Inc.
Lanham • Boulder • New York • Toronto • Oxford

ROWMAN & LITTLEFIELD PUBLISHERS, INC.

Published in the United States of America
by Rowman & Littlefield Publishers, Inc.
A wholly owned subsidiary of The Rowman & Littlefield Publishing Group, Inc.
4501 Forbes Boulevard, Suite 200, Lanham, Maryland 20706
www.rowmanlittlefield.com

P.O. Box 317, Oxford OX2 9RU, UK

British Library Cataloguing in Publication Information Available

Library of Congress Cataloging-in-Publication Data

Sullivan, Oriel, 1957–
    Changing gender relations, changing families : tracing the pace of change over time
/ Oriel Sullivan.
        p.   cm. — (The gender lens series)
    Includes bibliographical references and index.
    ISBN-13: 978-0-7425-4622-6 (cloth : alk. paper)
    ISBN 10: 0-7425-4622-5 (cloth : alk. paper)
    ISBN-13: 978-0-7425-4623-3 (pbk. : alk. paper)
    ISBN-10: 0-7425-4623-3 (pbk. : alk. paper)
    1. Sex role. 2. Sexual division of labor. 3. Family. I. Title. II. Series.
HQ1075.S83 2005
306.8701—dc22

                                                                              2005033514
Printed in the United States of America

♾™ The paper used in this publication meets the minimum requirements of American
National Standard for Information Sciences—Permanence of Paper for Printed Library
Materials, ANSI/NISO Z39.48-1992.

CONTENTS

)(

PART I
CHANGING THEORY

PART II
EVIDENCE FOR CHANGE

CONTENTS

PART III
CHANGING GENDER RELATIONS AT HOME

TABLES AND FIGURES

) (

Tables

Figures

PREFACE

) (

The conceptual basis for this book was many years in developing. Along the way I have published papers in academic journals, some sole- and some joint-authored, that contain some similar ideas or analyses. My grateful thanks go to my friends and collaborators Orly Benjamin and Jonathan Gershuny, whose insights, friendship, and collaboration have been hugely important in the development of the ideas expressed here. I would like to thank them specifically for their generosity in allowing me to rework material that is theirs too in conception. I am also indebted to Jonathan Gershuny for providing me with several specialized data sets from the Multinational Time Use Study, including those analyzed in chapters 4 and 5. Any errors of theory or substance remain of course my responsibility alone.

In addition I would like to express my thanks and appreciation to Barbara Risman, current editor of the Gender Lens series, who read carefully and commented critically on my manuscript, while at the same time giving me the encouragement I needed to believe that what I had to say was worth saying! My thanks also due to Christine Mallinson, who tried to help me understand more about current developments in feminist linguistics, and to a number of anonymous reviewers of the manuscript, who provided some thought-provoking and helpful suggestions.

PREFACE

Some of the material appearing in chapters 1, 2, 3, and 7 is a revised version of Sullivan 2004 and appears here with permission from Sage Publications and Sociologists for Women in Society.

Some of the material appearing in chapter 5 appeared previously in Sullivan 2000 and is reprinted here with kind permission from the British Sociological Association and Sage Publications.

INTRODUCTION
CHANGE—PROCESSES AND PACE

) (

Changing Gender Relations, Changing Families: Tracing the Pace of Change over Time is about changes in gender relations and practices in the home. These changes, in combination with larger shifts in the wider discursive environment, are, I argue, indicative of more far-reaching changes in gender relations.

A large body of literature is by now available on gender practices and relations around the issue of the domestic division of labor both within and between households.[1] However, with a few recent exceptions, relatively little of this literature takes as its central theme *processes of change* in these areas. The focus of this book is on changing domestic gender practices and relations among heterosexual couples, as evidenced on many different levels—from changes in attitudes about gender equality in the home to the quantitative analysis of change in the domestic division of labor. Indeed, one of the central contentions of the book is that the coincidence of evidence from many different levels of analysis should concentrate our attention on a theorization of change. For, despite the growing evidence for change, there has been a comparative absence from the literature of research that directly addresses the nature and significance of such change. The majority of literature in the area has focused instead on why gender inequalities in the home are so persistent. The reasons for this are, I argue, partly theoretical and partly connected to the nature of the empirical evidence that has been available. The phrases "the dual burden," "the second shift," and "the stalled revolution" are concepts that have made an important contribution to our understanding of inequalities in

1

domestic labor and related issues of gender power within the household. As such they have entered every respectable textbook on the subject. However, while as shorthand terms they punchily convey an important message, at the same time they have acted in the past as potent symbols for an argument for no meaningful change in domestic gender relations. For some time, I believe, this position had an overall negative impact on the development of research into the nature of, and possibilities for, change. In chapter 2, which is about conceptual and theoretical difficulties in the discussion of changing gender practices in the home, I explain and attempt to justify this contention.

With regard to the empirical evidence, practically all research conducted until very recently on the division of domestic labor has been based on cross-sectional data. Inevitably, the evidence looked (and looks) very bad since what we are used to seeing is a comparison of men's and women's contributions to domestic labor, and the discrepancy between them was, and is still, relatively enormous. Because of the size of this gap, even those studies that compared results with findings from earlier research often arrived at the same conclusion of very little evidence for meaningful change. My argument is that we have not taken either a *long enough* perspective or a *longitudinal* perspective on this question. Research on the gender division of domestic labor only really began in the 1960s with the rise of the women's movement and did not become a major research issue in family and gender studies until the 1970s. Consequently the basis for comparison between similar studies has in the main part been limited to a period of perhaps twenty-five years. The question is, what kind of change did we expect to see in twenty-five years? The expectation of a more dramatic change than we have witnessed in actuality was, I think, influenced by what Connell refers to as the "apocalyptic thinking" of the women's movement period (Connell 2000), which itself influenced and was influenced by a particular theoretical and political position on gender relations that is antithetical to the idea of gradualist change. This position had the effect that any change short of an upheaval in the structures of patriarchy could not really be considered a meaningful change.

The time has come perhaps to take a step back and consider the issue of change in gender practices and relations in the domestic sphere from a longer historical perspective, one that enables a different theoretical perspective on change. In this book I present the multilayered evidence for change, argue for an acceptance that change is with us, and offer a theoretical structure that can articulate those layers. The approach I develop makes connections between the wider discursive environment, affecting both the public and the private spheres, and the interactions and negotiations that individuals engage in on a day-to-day basis, with the focus on gender relations and practices in the domestic sphere. In conception it therefore belongs with what Risman (2004) identifies as the "more recent integrative approaches," which treat gender as a structure combining individual, interactional, and institutional dimensions. Within these approaches it is of course the combination of these different levels of analysis that represents the most challenging theoretical task. In this book I hope to show how processes of interaction among couples in the home are embedded in a recursive relationship within wider discursive structures, which they simultaneously are shaped by and help to construct. The central argument I hope to make is that we should be taking change seriously as a theoretical issue, not just in the public sphere but also in the domestic sphere. It is sometimes a difficult position to take, in the face both of current metaphors of rapid change ("runaway juggernauts"?; see chapter 2) and of a justified feminist critique of the pace of change in both the public and private spheres. But if meaningful change *is* occurring, as I believe it is, albeit slowly, then the theoretical tools to address it need to be developed.

Changing Gender Relations, Changing Families is structured in the following way: In chapter 1, I outline the theoretical elements that seem to me the most useful for developing an account of the processes of change in gender practices within the home, and in chapter 2 I discuss the theoretical inhibitions to the acceptance and investigation of these processes. The middle part of the book presents the empirical evidence for change both in elements of the wider discursive environment and in gender practices around the domestic division of labor, including the presentation of findings based on directly comparable cross-national data from the mid-1960s to the late 1990s. In the final part of the book, I outline the elements of a theoretical framework for understanding change in gender relations in the domestic sphere, based on the link between changes in the wider discursive context and microlevel processes of interaction in the home.

Note

1. It is beyond the scope of this book to provide a thorough review of this extensive literature, although I do refer to some of the main findings where it is relevant to the argument about change (e.g., chapter 5 on differences).

PART I
CHANGING THEORY

CHAPTER ONE
THEORIZING CHANGE

) (

Gender transformations in the public sphere in Western industrialized countries over the past few decades have been both widespread and widely acknowledged (although still problematic in the sense that they reveal changing patterns of equality and inequality in different areas over time and space—Walby 1997). The focus on change as evidenced in many recent texts has therefore been centered on the public sphere—on employment patterns and educational status; social and family policy; and most recently, on issues of citizenship (Morris and Lyon 1996; Berkovitch 1999; Crompton 1999). Strong theoretical emphasis has also been placed on the importance of women's political collective agency in transforming structures of patriarchy (Walby 1997). This focus has made an important contribution both to the general level of sensitivity to issues of gender inequality in the public sphere and in bringing a feminist awareness directly into the public arena.

Given the increasing recognition of the close links between the public and the domestic spheres and the growing significance of the public sphere in the regulation of the domestic, it would indeed be surprising if the changes that have taken place in the public sphere were not to some extent reflected in changes in gender practices and relations in the domestic sphere. This is the "weak version" of the argument for the existence of similar changes in the domestic sphere. The stronger argument is based on a growing body of literature documenting empirical evidence for changes in gender practices within the domestic sphere (as measured for example by the time spent on different domestic tasks), in which both the absolute and relative contribution of men is seen to be increasing over time. The debate lies in what such changes mean. Controversy still exists over whether these changes should be interpreted merely as adjustments occurring in response to changes in the public sphere (such as changes in women's employment) or as more meaningful indicators of change in gender ideologies and relations in the domestic sphere.

In any event, changes in the domestic sphere have received far less attention at a theoretical level than have changes in the public sphere, while at the same time the recent increase in writings on masculinity and fatherhood, together with the huge burgeoning of self-help/therapy discourses, brings with it intimations at least of wider transformations in personal relationships. In this book, I argue that these trends deserve more theoretical attention than has hitherto been given them in respect of their potential significance for change in gender practices and relations in the domestic sphere. In the section that follows, I outline a theoretical framework that makes connections between the wider discursive environment, affecting both the public and the private spheres, and the interactions and negotiations that individuals engage in on a day-to-day basis, with the focus on gender practices in the domestic sphere.

Elements of an Approach to Change: Doing Gender

As a theoretical starting point for the approach I present, I return to the idea of "doing gender" (Berk 1985; West and Zimmerman 1987; West and Fenstermaker 1993). The important point about the doing gender approach is that it involves the active (re)construction of gender in daily interaction. So by beginning here, at the level of interaction, I hope at the start to forestall the criticism that my argument about change implies a call for complacency. I do not conceive of the changes I describe as an *inevitable* process, disconnected somehow from the actions of acting subjects. It is clear that they have been struggled for, fought over, and hard won over decades, not only in the public and political arena but also in innumerable daily contestations and negotiations both in the home and outside it. Since the focus of this book is on the domestic sphere, I do not directly address the contribution of the feminist movement as a political force; but I do believe that many of the changes I describe, both at the discursive level and at the level of gender practice in the home, have been both directly and indirectly affected by the political efforts and action undertaken by the various forces of that movement. A great amount of political, emotional, and physical effort at all levels has been expended—an amount perhaps disproportionate to what has been achieved. But if these changes are to continue, then I believe that the same effort must continue to be expended, not least at the level of our daily interactions.

The doing gender perspective was developed during the 1980s, partly in response to the then current language of sex roles (i.e., in response to a static vision of essentialized sex roles in which the expected behaviors of the sexes were clearly defined and differentiated) (Connell 1987; Marx Ferree 1990). Instead, the doing gender perspective emphasized processes of "situated behavior," in which gender is continually being actively constructed and used in interaction. As such, the concept clearly provides potential for a theorization of the *production* of new gender relations and therefore for the theorization of change. Many presentations of the doing gender approach have directly addressed the potential of the perspective for examining alternative and changing constructions of gender—this being the case, for example, both of West and Zimmerman's classic presentation of 1987 and of Marx Ferree's 1990 review of the gender perspective in family research: "The gender perspective focuses attention on the continual struggles to maintain and change gender relations" (Marx Ferree 1990, 870).

According to the approach, for an individual woman or man the "accomplishment" of gender involves behaving in a way that is accountable to expectations of appropriate gender behavior. There is consequently always a reference to an existing set of normative guidelines regulating appropriate gender behavior. However, while the guidelines that regulate appropriate gender behavior are contingent, varying from time to time and from place to place, the main research emphasis has tended to be on the way doing gender reproduces existing normative constructions of gender (e.g., Berk 1985; DeVault 1991). There has been less direct discussion of the potential for developing alternative models of gender through the process of doing gender itself. Thus, in some presentations, including the classic discussion of Berk (1985), there is clear reference to the hopelessness of escaping the existing set of normative guidelines that regulate gendered behavior in the home. Two examples follow:

> If the "doing" of gender provides a framework by which husbands and wives reaffirm their relation to each other and to work . . . then departures from these normatively circumscribed ideals are ruled out. After all, "doing" gender serves to guide and thus limit the members, not to expand on already-complicated human affairs. (Berk 1985, 208)

> The production of household goods and services—and with it, the production of gender—may serve to thwart the efforts of any member to transform her or his household-work life. (209)

According to this take on the issue, therefore, change is unlikely to come from *within* the process of doing gender.

In other examples from the empirical exposition of the approach, while the possibilities for change may have been recognized, there is still emphasis on the regulatory nature of *existing* normative guidelines governing gender behavior in the home. For instance, normative conceptions of "essential womanliness" are shown to regulate the behavior of women of very different material circumstances (DeVault 1991, 203), while West and Fenstermaker describe gender as "conduct accountable to normative conceptions of womanly or manly natures" (1993, 152). While it is of course recognized that these normative conceptions can change, the implication is, as Berk argues, that such change is unlikely to come from within. Writing of the fusion in situated interaction of household work and gender, West and Fenstermaker argue that "the naturalness of each is reflexively defined by the other, and as a result of their accomplishment in concert, the equity of the arrangements they sustain is virtually impossible to question" (1993, 162).

In examples from later empirical research, such as that of Zvonkovic et al., the focus likewise has been on how a single set of normative guidelines concerning "appropriate" and "inappropriate" gender behavior is reconstructed. Zvonkovic et al. demonstrate how "couples generally tended to construct gender in their marriages in traditional ways, and the internal relationship processes were most often in consonance with traditional cultural norms and the structure of the gendered, paid work force" (Zvonkovic et al. 1996, 99). They "look forward" to research that addresses how marital couples can "enact lasting work-family solutions that are not in consonance with traditional expectations, and how couples can construct gender in marriages in a way that can change the larger society" (99).

So while there is a recognized theoretical potential for an approach to change based on interaction within the doing gender perspective, the main thrust of research (at least until recently) has tended to be on how contextual behaviors lead to the reproduction of existing structures of gender inequality, rather than on their possible contribution to processes of differentiation and change in those structures. In other words, the doing gender approach provides an enabling framework for addressing change, *but* the major research emphasis has tended to be on the interactive (re)construction of traditional normative models of gender. This is in line with a general, and justifiable, tendency within modernist feminist theory over the last thirty years to focus mainly on the reproduction within the home of existing gender inequalities.

Therefore, as a second theoretical element in the approach I am presenting here, I argue that it may be helpful to combine the potential of the emphasis on daily interaction and negotiation of the doing gender approach with a theoretical frame in which the *conditions* for the accomplishment of change within interaction are explicitly addressed. One such frame is provided by the concept of "gender consciousness," as discussed in Gerson and Peiss (1985).

Elements of an Approach to Change: Gender Consciousness

Gender consciousness is described by Gerson and Peiss (1985) as a continuum, at one end of which a generalized awareness of gender issues may be succeeded by a full consciousness of the rights associated with specific gender locations. The development of gender consciousness thus involves a process including a growing recognition of rights. The conditions under which this consciousness develops depend partly on information from the wider society. For example, the rise of feminism provided new conditions for an awareness of rights and thus for the development of gender consciousness. Gender consciousness may therefore be utilized as a means of describing the potential for change in the domestic sphere in the light of new emphases on intimacy and equality in personal relationships because these discourses provide new conditions and information for the development of a consciousness of rights. But, crucially, day-to-day social interaction also influences the development of an awareness of rights. Gender relations are therefore linked to gender consciousness via the active generation of rights in social interaction (which may of course be either reactionary or progressive in nature). According to Thompson (1993), gender consciousness thus constitutes a central component of our understanding of women's attempts at change.

The concept of gender consciousness as used by Gerson and Peiss may therefore be utilized as a means of describing the potential for change in the domestic sphere in the light of the new emphasis on discourses of intimacy and equality (see Cancian 1987). These discourses provide new conditions and information for the development of a consciousness not only of rights but also of responsibilities. So in this perspective, women's attempts at change take place in a context not just of a growing recognition of rights but also in a context of a (perhaps more slowly) growing awareness of reciprocal responsibilities on the part of men (as the more privileged group). In addition, these discourses can provide access for some women to specific interactional tools that may become direct, active resources in the accomplishment of change. In other words, it may be possible to connect arguments about the new discourses of equality, marital power (arising from differential access to resources), and the development of gender consciousness for both men and women. These arguments are more fully developed in chapters 6 and 7.

Summary and Conclusion

In summary, I am proposing an integrative approach to understanding changing gender relations that centers on the linking together of an account based on the analysis of daily interaction, negotiation, and struggle with a concept of changing gender consciousness. This involves the development of a multilevel theoretical frame that can link changes in the wider discursive sphere to processes of change as they occur in interaction between men and women in the domestic sphere. On the one hand, it is critical to identify changes at the level of the ideologies and discourses that structure gendered interaction. On the other, at the microlevel, the key lies in the detailed analysis of interactive processes of change as described by the actors themselves. Women's and men's day-to-day negotiations and struggles around the domestic division of labor can be conceived within such a framework as part of a wider social process that involves slow changes in both consciousness and practices. In this way it becomes possible to incorporate into the theoretical frame a recognition of the simultaneously *constituted* and *constitutive* nature of day-to-day interaction, into which dynamic elements of change are being introduced at different levels of the analysis.

Risman (1998, 2004) refers to four social science research traditions in the explanation of gender: gendered personalities; social structural explanations; doing gender; and the current integrative approaches, which treat gender as a "socially constructed stratification system" (2004, 430). I would locate my approach, as she locates her gender structure model, in this fourth category. In the recognition of the mutually constituted and constitutive nature of action and structure and the attempt to theorize their interrelations, a debt is owed both to Giddens's theory of structuration (Giddens 1984) and to Bourdieu's notion of habitus (Bourdieu 1984). Where I differ from Risman's approach is that I put more emphasis on the transformative potential of everyday interaction.

In the construction of her gender structure model, Risman focuses on three interpenetrating dimensions: the individual level of gendered identities, gendered cultural meanings and expectations as played out in interaction, and gender-specific institutional constraints and opportunities (Risman 1998, 2004). I distinguish her second level (cultural meanings and expectations as played out in interaction) into two analytic components—cultural meanings, norms, and expectations on the one hand and interactive processes on the other. The purpose is both to emphasize and to facilitate analysis of how cultural meanings, norms, and expectations can be challenged, resisted, revised, and eventually changed in the ongoing processes of interaction. For while I am in agreement that, for the most part, the processes of doing gender in daily interaction will reproduce and concretize existing hegemonic inequalities, given the right conditions they also contain within them the potential for (a slow kind of) change. Indeed one of the aims of this book is to outline some of these conditions. Therefore I do not agree with Risman that we have come as far as we can with incremental change and will have to undergo a period of "gender vertigo," as she suggests, in order to arrive at a transformation of the gender structure. As I have already hinted, I believe that change can be slow and piecemeal yet still in the end effect a radical transformation if we take the longer perspective—in this sense I have a more optimistic view of slow, incremental change. I return to the important contrast between revolutionary and incremental views of change in chapter 2.

The following chapter addresses what I see to have been the theoretical inhibitions to the analysis of change in gender practices and relations in the domestic sphere. I begin with a discussion of the meaning and nature of change, since it can be argued that much of our ongoing theoretical difficulty with the notion of change in the domestic sphere stems from two particular modernist takes on the nature of change. The first of these is a vision of change associated with the literature on late modernity. The second is a structuralist argument about the absence of meaningful change in gender practices and relations in the home. In combination (and there is a connection between them), I argue that these positions inhibited the growth until very recently of the development of a body of theory focusing on the accomplishment of change.

SLOW NATURE OF CHANGE, SLOW CHANGE IN THEORY

) (

The theoretical literature on late modernity contains some peculiarly apocalyptic visions of change. Large-scale upheavals and dramatic changes are presented as characteristic of late modernity, a perspective that is made explicit in the choice of metaphors such as "juggernauts," "volcanoes," and the "runaway society" (Giddens 1990; Beck, Giddens, and Lasch 1994). Such metaphors dramatize size and speed. The perception of the nature of change that they support and reflect is that only large and dramatic change really constitutes change. This perspective is, I argue, in keeping with the masculinist tradition of classical history, in which large and dramatic *moments* of change (wars, revolutions, coups, elections, market busts and booms, and other upheavals) are regarded as the material from which history is made (for a critique of modernist historical sociology, see Stones 1996). However, these moments of dramatic change may be contrasted with other less dramatic but equally meaningful changes that go largely unrecorded in the pages of classical history but that have informed the content of feminist and social history. I refer to the small social and economic changes affecting the real-life circumstances of individuals on a day-to-day basis—accumulating slowly, practiced and contested in daily interaction—that amount in the end to substantial and substantive change.

So in contrast to metaphors of rapid, dramatic change, I argue in this book for the significance of change based on a different metaphor, of a slow dripping of change, perhaps unnoticeable from year to year but that in the end is persistent enough to lead to the slow dissolution of previously existing structures. In these sorts of changes, daily practices and interactions both reflect and are constitutive of attitudes and discourse, in processes that stretch perhaps over generations. These changes *are* important, but we should not expect too much from them in a short period of time. Along similar lines, in a section titled *The Historical Moment*, Connell (2000) makes the point that we now all recognize that the "apocalyptic thinking" of the period of the women's liberation movement was naive—but that nevertheless we now increasingly accept the historicity of social transformations in gender.

However, it is the idea of revolutionary change, interpreted as the rapid, large-scale upheaval of structures, that has had the most profound influence on modernist thinking on the nature of change. And the conceptual problem with this way of thinking carried to its extreme—the idea that only revolution can bring meaningful change—is that it makes it impossible to consider any other sort of change as really meaningful (for an extreme example of the insistence on the essential stability of historical structures, see Eisenstadt 1978). There is a parallel here with the different versions of Marxist analysis of the historical development of welfare policy. In the classical version of Marxist theory, only revolution can bring a true transformation in capitalist structures and relations. Other forms of change (e.g., the introduction of better working and living conditions) are simply measures designed to placate the working classes, to engender false consciousness, and thus to ward off revolution. To put it simply, there is no real change apart from revolutionary change. According to this argument, resistance (on the small scale) is useless.

In other versions of Marxist theory, however, there is a recognition of the significance of smaller changes struggled over and finally won by the working classes, which in the end can amount to meaningful transformations in structure. Some authors have argued that in the creation of the British Welfare State over the first part of the twentieth century, we can see an example of this latter process (e.g., Saville 1975). The idea of revolutionary change has also had a profound influence on the development of feminist theory, reaching its peak perhaps in the 1970s and 1980s simultaneously with the rise of academic Marxism in Europe.

Slow Change in Theory

In the early burgeoning of second-wave feminist writing in the late 1970s and 1980s, emphasis was put on detailing patterns of employment segregation according to gender, on the identification of housework as labor, and on the unequal gender division of such labor. This literature provided a counterargument to the idea of the "symmetrical family" (see Smart and Neale 1999) and made a significant contribution both to the definition of household labor as work (Oakley 1974) and to the construction of theories of structured inequality in gender relations (e.g., Lupri 1983). While there has been subsequently an increasing recognition of change in some of the components of gender inequality in the public sphere (see, for example, Crompton 1999; Morris and Lyon 1996; Lorber 1994), there has been among many feminist authors a certain reluctance to take on board the possibility of meaningful change in gender relations within the domestic sphere. This is so despite the fact that the definition of housework as unpaid *work* (Oakley 1974), as opposed to a fulfillment of a naturalized role, theoretically opened the way both for the conceptualization of the relations between paid and unpaid labor and to the possibility of changing gendered labor relations in the domestic as well as in the public sphere. In the face of findings documenting changes in the relative contributions of men and women to domestic work, the question "So what?" was asked—in other words, do these changes add anything new to our theoretical understanding of unequal domestic gender relations (Smart and Neale 1999)? The most influential argument in the literature on this subject over the 1980s and 1990s was that, although we might perceive some small changes around the edges of the performance of domestic labor, the overwhelming evidence points to a persistence in existing unequal gender relations (see, for example, Hochschild 1989, 1997; Morris 1990; Warde and Hetherington 1993; Lorber 1994; Jamieson 1998; Hearn 1999).

However, over the same period, in both Europe and North America a growing body of empirical findings documented changes in the relative contribution of women and men to household work. Partly as a response to the initial documentation of such changes, more research attention was focused on issues such as the *management* and *responsibility* for household work (as opposed to its performance); on understandings of equity, entitlement, and gratitude in domestic labor, posing the important question how a myth of "fairness" can be maintained in the face of obvious ongoing inequality (Bittman and Lovejoy 1993; Hochschild 1989; Pyke and Coltrane 1996; Sanchez and Kane 1996; Thompson 1991); and, in the

North American literature in particular, on the sociopsychological media-tors and consequences (e.g., marital quality) of inequity in household la-bor allocations (e.g., Lennon and Rosenfield 1994; Voydanoff and Donnelly 1999). Another major area of research has been concerned with identifying *differences* in the pattern of household labor between subgroups of the population according to demographic (e.g., age; ethnicity; marital status; number, age, and sex of children), social (e.g., class; education; sex-ual preference), or economic (e.g., absolute or relative income; relative hours of work) factors. However, despite a large body of literature on ex-isting differences, there has been relatively little analysis of longitudinal *trends* (although see Spitze 1986 for an early example) or processes of change.

The careful and critical documentation of historical inequalities in household labor; the teasing out of the relationships between task per-formance, task management, and feelings of entitlement and gratitude around the domestic division of labor; and the analysis of how inequity af-fects life quality resulting from this body of research have made a huge contribution to our understanding of these important processes. But in much of this literature (and perhaps for good reasons), the main empha-sis was on how gendered inequalities in domestic labor have been sus-tained and reinforced. The result was, ironically, that an interesting and uneasy agreement existed between some reactionary positions associated with the backlash against feminism (a conservative "no meaningful change" position based on the inevitability of essentialized roles—see for example Dench 1999) and some of the feminist literature that has argued the same, but from an entirely different theoretical perspective.

My intention is not to criticize either the motivations or the origins of the "no meaningful change" argument,[1] which should perhaps be ex-pressed as "no meaningful change short of an upheaval in existing struc-tures." It coincided with a set of political and theoretical contingencies that made it the most effective perspective at that time. Moreover, the contribution of many of the authors who took this view to the develop-ment of feminist research in the domestic sphere has been of enormous significance. Nevertheless, I argue that some of the theoretical underpin-nings of the early feminist research agenda have acted to inhibit for a con-siderable time the understanding and development of a theorization of change.

So what were these theoretical underpinnings, and why did they have an inhibiting effect on the discussion of change in the domestic sphere? For, as Pleck has noted, theoretical stances about the extent and nature of changes in the domestic sphere, in particular the argument against the existence (or not) of meaningful change, have reflected deeply rooted beliefs (Pleck 1993; see also Jamieson 1999). To comprehend this effect better, I think it is necessary first to distinguish between the theoretical viewpoints of structured patriarchy, as developed in the 1970s within socialist feminism, and the gender perspective, developing from the 1980s, that emphasized more processual, relational ways of thinking. This distinction can be related to the more general distinction I made previously about ways of conceptualizing change.

In the early stages of the development of feminist theory in the 1970s, there was a strong (and politically necessary—Lorber 1994) ideological commitment to the identification and description of patriarchal relations. However, the theory of structured patriarchy, carried to its logical conclusion, suggests that no really meaningful change in gender relations can be conceived of without a fundamental upheaval in the structured gender inequality associated with patriarchal social relations. This was always a thorny dilemma within socialist and radical feminism debate (e.g., Barrett 1997). The argument for no meaningful change in the domestic sphere therefore developed within a set of political and theoretical contingencies that made it the most effective position for the time.

At the same time, exchange theory and the middle-level theories deriving from it (such as relative resources—Brines 1994) were appearing regularly in the empirical literature to help explain domestic labor allocations (see Coltrane 2000). Where household labor practices are seen as changing directly in response to the movement toward greater equality for women in the public sphere, such models carry an underlying implication of progressive change. The major feminist criticism has been that such models do not sufficiently address existing structural inequalities in gender power and thus questions of constraint.

The last few years have seen a shift in emphasis on the subject of change in the gender literature. I use the term *gender literature* here as something newer and distinct from a feminist literature primarily focused on women's lives and experience. There is significance in this shift since many of the arguments I have used in the development of my approach to change have emerged from the more relationally based perspective of gender, including within it much of the recently burgeoning literature on masculinities. That the literature on masculinities and men should contain a more positive view about change might, of course, be dismissed on the grounds that men, as the more privileged group, are more likely to perceive small changes as meaningful (a glass being half full as opposed to half empty), in contrast to the perspective of the less privileged group.

However, writers about men are by no means in agreement that change is occurring. For example, describing himself as a "materialist structuralist," McMahon has recently written that evidence on change in the domestic division of labor should, far from being understood optimistically, be seen in terms of "a largely successful male resistance" (1999, 7). I would take issue with McMahon on several counts in respect of both the evidence he presents and with the interpretation made of it, but I refer to it here in illustration of the previous point. My general argument is that the literature on gender (and on masculinities within this) has not been bound in the same way by a preexisting theoretical climate that has been skeptical of the idea of change (see Zalewski 2000 on some of the effects of the theoretical orthodoxies of modernist feminism).

But whatever the reason, the single most significant shift in emphasis in much of the literature over the last decade is an increasing recognition of change toward a position of greater equality in households, at least in the division of domestic tasks. We might describe this as a widespread recognition of a change in *behavior*, significant certainly for the women who have experienced it, but since it might occur on an ad hoc basis in response to practical contingencies (such as a wife moving into full-time employment), not *necessarily* indicating deeper change at the level of gender ideologies and structures. However, there are also increasing signs of agreement that we are in the throes of a more significant change at this latter level. Following the development of the gender perspective and a more sociopsychological approach in the North American literature, there is now a more grounded body of situated, processual theory to support this conclusion. An early optimistic account suggests that "the critical mass of conditions, situations, and actions is viewed to be present to implant an irrevocable change in the mind, consciousness and soul of humankind" (Lewis and Sussman 1986, xiii).

Other writers have, perhaps wisely, been more circumspect. For example, Segal has written about the current slow pace of change—but does not doubt that the possibilities exist for a long-run transformation. The difficulties are how to generate pressure for it and how to recognize its preconfigurations (Segal 1990). Like Jamieson, I would suggest that we are in the middle of "the flux and confusion of an uneven transition" (1999, 489).

However, while being skeptical of an ongoing adherence to the argument of no meaningful change, it is also necessary to avoid a naive focus on change, carrying with it progressive and evolutionary connotations of movement toward full equality. Processes of change are more complex, contingent, and conflictual than this. Therefore, in accordance with a general shift within the gender literature toward a growing emphasis on issues of plurality, resistance, and shifting constructions of identity, we need to develop models of change that can incorporate the complexity of the intersection between ideology, attitudes, and practice in situated, located contexts. Such perspectives need to be able to address the tension between the growing cultural emphasis on intimacy in personal relationships and the continuing structural bolstering of gender inequality within the domestic sphere. At a wider level, a dialectic process between social policies affecting families and changes that may be occurring in intimate relationships must also be addressed. And all these changes are happening within a context in which women are increasingly moving into the public sphere in ways that impinge directly on the private (Morris and Lyon 1996; Crompton 1996; Walby 1997).

Appearing recently in the literature have been examples of analytical frameworks attempting to address the interwoven relationships between some of these elements. Connell's concept of configurations of gender practice, for example, gives recognition to the constitutive nature of action—masculinity and femininity are regarded from this perspective as "dynamic processes of configuring practice through time, which transform their starting points in gender structure" (2000, 28). Another example is Risman's analysis of the gender structure, which, she writes, is a human invention and thus subject to change: "Even though gender structure is powerful, it is not determinative . . . as individuals and families develop new ways to live, the gender structure itself evolves. . . . [Thus] actors shape the gender structure they inherit" (1998, 5).

Summary and Conclusion

So we do see appearing in the literature on gender the beginnings of the possibility of a full theorization of change. It is to this area that I hope to contribute in this book, first by outlining and then by specifying some of the connections between daily interaction and the wider discursive context. Before taking up in more detail the development of the theoretical frame, I present some of the main elements of the evidence for change. Of course, inevitably, the kind of evidence that is considered significant is intimately linked to the particular model of change. In an approach that attempts to combine a focus on interaction with a recognition of the constitutive nature of the structural level, all existing within a wider discursive environment, the scope for such evidence is large and multilayered. In part II of this book on the evidence for change, I present a "slice" through these layers, ranging from changes in the wider discursive environment to changes in gender practices in the domestic sphere.

The next three chapters are arranged as follows: In chapter 3, I address some changing aspects of the wider discursive environment—attitudinal and linguistic changes indicative both of shifting gender ideologies and practices, together with the evidence for change in images of masculinity, particularly of fatherhood. In the subsequent two chapters, I present quantitative empirical evidence for change in the time spent by men and women on various kinds of unpaid work within the home from the 1960s to the 1990s. Chapter 4 focuses on large-scale cross-national trends, and chapter 5, in keeping with the increasing emphasis on difference, analyzes a study of *changing differences* in the division of domestic labor between particular subgroups of the British population, defined according to employment and class characteristics. The final part of the book (part III) focuses on processes of changing gender relations in the domestic sphere.

Note

1. I am wary of labeling this argument a "position." A position perhaps implies a concerted, directly explicated set of theoretical arguments with a common view and aim, and this is not necessarily the case in relation to no meaningful change.

PART II
EVIDENCE FOR CHANGE

THE DISCURSIVE CONTEXT: ATTITUDES, LANGUAGE, AND MASCULINITIES

) (

In part II of this book, I address some of the elements of the multi-layered evidence for change. This evidence, although now increasingly accepted, is still contested at various levels. Taken separately, some of the changes do not appear to be large or rapid. Thus we can talk about slow changes over time in attitudes toward gender equality, movements in the direction of gender-neutral language use, and the appearance among certain groups of a new conception of "caring fatherhood." Similarly, in studies of time use within households we can detect a few minutes extra time contributed by husbands to domestic labor over a decade; an increase of several percentage points in the percentage of couples devoting an equal share of time to domestic work; and a small response in terms of time contributed to housework by husbands whose wives take jobs outside the home. However, it is the coincidence in the direction of change between these different levels of evidence—the discursive and the quantitative—that provides the strongest argument for meaningful change and for the necessity to address such change theoretically.

In this chapter I discuss evidence that deals specifically with *changes* in some elements of the wider discursive context: in gender attitudes, language, and images of masculinity. I have selected these topics from among many others both because they represent significant elements of the wider discursive environment (attitudes, discourse, and symbolic representations) and because I am familiar with literature in each area that documents slow but meaningful change. Since research in each of these areas is extensive and complex, I have also, inevitably, been selective in my choice of examples and arguments. My purpose is to show the importance of slow change as demonstrated from significant research in each area. First, I discuss the evidence for change in gender attitudes. Subsequently I address the significance of changing language, and finally I discuss some of the literature on changing masculinities, in particular evidence for changes in the symbolic representations and behaviors associated with fatherhood. This sequence is arbitrary, for among and between these elements lies an entangled web of reciprocal causality. Discussion of the picking apart and (re)ordering of these elements is a theme that runs throughout the chapter.

Knijn (1995) suggests that transformations in social relations are caused by wider social processes, which may perhaps be given direction by particular social movements. The influence of the feminist movement on the social processes I describe in this book has been profound. But I directly address in this chapter mainly those wider social processes, even though, for example, feminist activists have been to the forefront in the definition and application of nonsexist language.

Chapters 4 and 5 focus on a different slice of the multilayered evidence and address quantitative empirical evidence for change in the domestic division of labor on a cross-national basis over a thirty-year time span. I argue that the scale of the trends and, especially, their consistency do indeed point in the direction of meaningful change.

Changing Attitudes

The most widely reported-on aspect of the discursive environment is attitudes (or, in different formulations, *values* or *ideals*). However, the relationship between attitudes and behavior is notoriously difficult to disentangle. Attitudes can be perceived as intermediate variables occupying the complex and interwoven space between discourse and behavior (see Baxter 1992; Crompton and Harris 1999), but the direction of causality in this space is not necessarily clear. For example, do changes in attitudes to gender in the domestic sphere merely echo changes in behavior that might arise from a rational choice model of household strategies in response to greater employment opportunities for women, or can changing attitudes and values themselves generate new behaviors? In a reverse of the normal assumption, and following Caplan (1987), one of the contributors to the debate has observed that "the assumption that behavior follows values is often naïve: more often values and norms follow modal behavior" (Hofstede 1998, 160). Another major author in the area has subsequently posed the question "so why study attitudes?" (Scott 1999). Answering her own question, and noting the congruence between attitude change in relation to divorce and changing patterns of family structure, Scott suggests that while attitudes are not *necessarily* good indicators of behavior they do "help constitute the climate of opinion against which behaviours are judged" (74). So while evidence for change in attitudes in itself does not *necessarily* mean that change in gender relations at home is occurring (i.e., it is not sufficient evidence for such change), we might well from a theoretical perspective consider it a *necessary* condition for meaningful change.

The association between attitudes to gender equality and the division of domestic labor is by now well established using large-scale data (see, for example, Goldscheider and Waite 1991). In general, those men and women whose attitudes to gender equality are more positive (*liberal* or *progressive* in other formulations) tend to share domestic work more equally. The same relationship also appears to be true of systems of household financial management. For example, Vogler (1994) reports that the attitude of the husband (sexist or nonsexist) is the most important factor in determining the control and management of financial matters in the home. However, despite the large volume of research on the attitudes toward work and family roles, relatively few large-scale studies have attempted to assess *changes* in attitudes and values using consistent and comparable measures over time. The majority of these studies have been conducted in single countries, for example in the United States (e.g., Losh-Hesselbart 1988; Thornton 1989; Willinger 1993) and Britain (e.g., Dex 1988; Scott 1999), but a few have also made cross-national comparisons of change. Among the earliest of these cross-national comparisons (in terms of the period surveyed) is a review of changes in values over the 1980s by Inglehart (1997) based on the World Values Survey. Using more recent data, Scott, Alwin, and Brown (1996) provide cross-national comparisons of attitudes featuring several European countries based on large-scale surveys for the 1990s. Since my focus is on change, it is on these cross-national studies that I concentrate.

The majority of the research on attitudes and values conducted in the 1980s found a movement toward a rejection of traditionally defined gender roles (the usual format in which the issue was then described). This has taken the form of a greater acceptance of nonfamilial roles for women, particularly among younger women with higher levels of education, and a rather less clear movement toward acceptance of a more familial role for men. Within this body of work, relatively less attention was directed toward the attitudes of men. However, an analysis by Losh-Hesselbart that compared attitudes of both men and women using national survey data from the United States shows that between 1977 and 1985 both sexes and all ages came to endorse more independent, less domestic roles for women. The attitude change reported among women was twice that for men (Losh-Hesselbart 1988). In a study of male college students' attitudes toward women's and men's family and work roles in the United States during the 1980s, Willinger concluded that the attitudes of young, well-educated men "suggest that the climate of opinion shifted in favor of gender equality" (1993, 127).

One of the aims of Scott, Alwin, and Brown (1996) was to investigate whether changes of this kind continued into the 1990s. Using cross-national comparative data sets, they investigated three types of gender-related beliefs and attitudes: the consequences of women working; gender ideology; and the importance of paid work. They found different patterns of change emerging across different countries, and they speculate as to how these differences may be related to (1) patterns of female employment, (2) the consciousness-raising effects of the women's movement, and (3) the relative emphasis on individual autonomy. For example, in a three-way comparison of the United States, Britain, and Germany, it is suggested that the particularly slow rate of change in attitudes among women in Britain is related to structural factors such as the high rates of part-time employment, involving juggling home and paid work responsibilities. These sorts of associations are supported by various recent cross-national studies. For example, in an examination of gender attitudes in Britain, Norway, and Czechoslovakia, Norwegians emerged as the most progressive, a finding that is attributed to the high profile on gender equality evident in Norwegian public life (Crompton and Harris 1999). From the same study, more liberal gender attitudes were associated with less traditional domestic divisions of labor within countries, while controlling for relevant socioeconomic and demographic factors. Likewise, Hofstede's index of masculinity (based on a range of fourteen work goals) identifies the

Scandinavian countries as having the lowest scores (i.e., the least conformist to definitions of hegemonic masculinity) of the fifty-three countries examined (Hofstede 1998).

The overall conclusion drawn by Scott, Alwin, and Brown is that, despite intercountry and cross-time variations, "the ideology surrounding traditional gender roles is increasingly rejected, though there is evidence that the pace of change has slowed in the 1990s" (1996, 489). They note that "women have been much more prepared than men to reject traditional gender role attitudes" (489). However, they also report that within-cohort change has been more rapid recently among men, at least in Britain. With respect to this point, which bears upon how we can interpret the change being observed, an important distinction must be made between change that occurs *within* cohorts (i.e., reflecting change in attitudes or behavior over an individual's lifetime), which may be more revolutionary in character, and change that occurs *between* cohorts (i.e., in a process of cohort succession, where younger generations replace older ones). Within-cohort, or intracohort, change implies a more rapid process, in which individuals display changing values or behavior over time, as opposed to a process of generational succession in attitudes represented by between-cohort, or intercohort, change. In Inglehart's 1997 study, for example, the claim is for widespread *inter*generational shifts in values (of which the move toward gender equality is one). However, Scott, Alwin, and Brown find that while gender ideology still shows big differences between cohorts, a significant proportion of change (40 to 60 percent) in Britain, the United States, and Germany over the period from the 1970s has been due to *intra*cohort changes. Although there was variation from decade to decade, the general finding that up to 60 percent of attitude change can be attributed to intracohort change is an important one since it implies a more rapid process of change, in which the same individuals display changing attitudes over time (Scott, Alwin, and Brown 1996).

To reemphasize the point from the British data, Scott, Alwin, and Brown conclude that there has been a recent (during the 1990s) increase in the percentage of change in men's attitudes due to *intra*cohort change—which suggests that recent changes in men's attitudes have been more dramatic than those for women, even though those for women have overall been greater (see also Scott 1999). Scott also makes the point that in relation to observed changes in attitudes toward, for example, abortion and divorce, changes in gender ideology still appear relatively small.

So we return to one of the original difficult questions about how much change is meaningful. How much of a change in attitudes would we expect to see reflected in (or reflecting) changing gendered practices in the domestic sphere? I have already referred to the difficulties of assessing the relationship between attitudes and behavior, and only a few authors directly discuss the question of causality at a theoretical level. Scott, Alwin, and Brown appear to support a causal relationship when they contend that "shifts in public attitudes can undoubtedly facilitate as well as reflect social change" (1996, 475). Similarly, Inglehart, in his evolutionary review of the World Values Survey focusing on the shift from modern to postmodern values, makes the rather more indirect assertion that "one cannot understand social change without taking [value systems] into account" (1997, 52), which implies but does not directly assert the existence of a causal relationship.

Willinger, who concluded that a general shift did occur in the climate of opinion among male college students in the 1980s, does directly address the theoretical issue. She argues that her conclusions lend support to a "cultural lag" theory of behavioral change in this area, in which attitudes manifest among higher social groups will eventually be reflected in both the attitudes and behaviors of all subgroups of the population (Willinger 1993). While many entertain doubts about the implication of inevitability implicit in cultural lag theory, it does nevertheless seem clear that most analysts in the area share the opinion that there has been a significant shift in attitudes related to gender ideology evident on a cross-national basis, and this shift is likely to continue. In addition, the relationship between behavior and attitudes, while complex, is seen to be real. That is to say, whatever the intricacies of the causal relationship, changes in attitudes are believed, at the least, to be manifest in changing behavior.

Changing Language

I turn now to the issue of changing language. Language and changes in it, like changes in attitudes, are associated in a complex causal loop with changes in other behaviors. Indeed, language is regarded by feminist linguists today as one of the elements that actively manifest and construct such changes (e.g., Eckert and McConnell-Ginet 2003). Language constitutes an integral part of daily interaction, and the pivot of my recursive model of change in domestic gender relations and practices (elaborated in part III) is daily interaction in the home. Linguistic practices and changes in linguistic representations therefore are significant elements in the theoretical framework that I present. This issue also has relevance to the discussion in chapter 6, where I introduce the example of therapeutic discourses.

The recognition that language does not simply reflect, but actively constitutes, social reality originated from the structural linguistic tradition associated with Saussure. This recognition has had huge significance for the development of research on linguistic representations and language production. However, recent feminist perspectives have challenged the structuralist model as tending to abstract from the crucial considerations of social practice, social context, and historical change (Zalewski 2000). Following the development of "speech act" theory, describing how verbal utterances are tantamount to actions (e.g., Austin 1962; Searle 1969), and the treatment by authors such as Giddens (1984) of language as a significant social process in the discursive reproduction of inequality, recent feminist sociolinguistic research is characterized by the studying of language as a social practice embedded within a social context (Hall and Bucholtz 1995; Eckert and McConnell-Ginet 2003). In this perspective, linguistic changes not only reflect changes in social constructs and identities but also actively participate in breaking down and reconstituting them (Bucholtz, Liang, and Sutton 1999).

Fraser (1997) makes the following observations about the potential of this kind of approach for feminist theorizing. First, "it treats discourses as contingent, positing that they arise, alter and disappear over time" (386). Second, it is concerned with how "people do things with words" (386), allowing us to view speakers as socially situated agents. Third, there is an assumption of a plurality of available discourses, contributing to a conception of individual identities that are not monolithic in character. Changing language is therefore seen as intimately connected to a discussion of changing gender relations. For example, according to Bucholtz, "Recent trends in feminist theory, and in social theory more generally, have made explicit the role of language in shaping, reproducing and challenging power relations" (1996, 267). On the same theme, in his description of language as one of the four aspects of a structure of gender relations, Connell states:

> The process of communication is increasingly recognized as a vital element of social processes. The symbolic structures called into play in communication—grammatical and syntactic rules, visual and sound vocabularies etc.—are important sites of gender practice. (Connell 2000, 26)

In her discussion and review of the state of feminism after postmodernism, Zalewski devotes considerable attention to the importance of language. She writes, with homage to Foucault, that language is one of the ways that power produces truth: Hence "names are vastly important" (2000, 59). Thus we know, for example, that in a process of "semantic inversion" (Smitherman 1977) both the names *nigger* and *queer* have been appropriated and reconstituted as positives as part of an active resistance by the communities they were applied to (as derogatory) in the 1950s and 1960s. As Kitzinger (2001), among others, has pointed out, slang terms are particularly amenable to change since slang is a primarily spoken and particularly dynamic language that evolves rapidly to meet current and specific cultural knowledges.

The tradition of feminist research into the gendered processes of language expanded after the rise of second-wave feminism in the 1960s and had strong links in its early development to the broader field of sociolinguistics, founded on the recognition that language is a social product. Language was therefore seen as rooted in gender ideology, leading to influential research on how language reflects gender inequality via, for example, pejorative naming terms (e.g., *doll*, *whore*) and the pervasiveness in most European languages of the generic masculine to express things both male and female (e.g., *chairman*, *mankind*). In addition, the language used by specific groups is seen not only to reflect but also to reproduce their social position. Lakoff (1975) observed how the differences between men's language and women's language reinforces gender inequalities. Much subsequent research was directed to describing differences in the linguistic behavior of men and women (e.g., Spender 1980; Coates 1986). More recent approaches, including conversation analysis, have put more emphasis on the details of the research context, or "talk-in-interaction" (e.g., Kitzinger 1998), and of individual variation *within* as well as across gender categories (Bucholtz 1999). In addition, there is a new and growing body of literature on the significance of language in the active construction of identity (e.g., Hall and Bucholtz 1995; Bucholtz, Liang, and Sutton 1999). This development occurred in parallel with the move in gender studies toward a performance-focused approach (as in "doing gender") and has led language and gender scholars to explore how linguistic performances actively construct both conventional gendered identities and identities that resist and challenge gender norms (see, for example, Eckhert and McConnell-Ginet 2003; Bucholtz and Hall 2004).

If we focus specifically on language changes in the area of gender, a carefully detailed book by Curzan (2003) describes the shifts that have occurred over time in the English language in relation to gender. In particular, she addresses the use of the generic masculine pronoun *he* and the prescriptive efforts made over several previous centuries to formalize its usage. In an early review of post–second-wave efforts to challenge English usage in relation to gender, Penfeld describes how the active political struggle to make the language more equal focused initially on linguistic aspects such as pronouns and vocabulary. Later, strategies for empowerment in mixed-sex interaction also received attention. Penfeld notes that, at this stage, "women began to take an active part in defining themselves both individually and collectively" (1987, xv). Feminists sought linguistic strategies for resisting current language forms and creating new ones as part of a process of the construction of new identities.

Zalewski (2000) writes that from the postmodern perspective it is important to understand how and in what circumstances word meanings are open to change via challenge and redefinition. She gives the example of the word *nigger* but might equally well have chosen *lady*. The question of changing word meanings is directly relevant to the link between changes in language, attitudes, and behavior, as research in linguistic relativity tells us: "As a community's beliefs, assumptions, concepts and practices change, so its lexicon changes to reflect them" (Clark 1996, 342).

At the same time, in a recursive relationship, the use of specific linguistic forms actively participates in the constitution and the maintenance of social constructs. So, for example, changes such as the fading from prominence of overtly sexist or racist language are not simply meaningless fads (as the backlash opponents of political correctness like to believe). To recognize the decline in usage of terms such as *lady*, the increase in references to *partner*, and the substitution of *humankind* for *mankind* is not to claim that sexism has vanished, just as the declining use of *nigger* is not to claim that racism has vanished, but instead to suggest that these changes in language use may be indicative of certain shifts in consciousness, ideology, and practice that go together with the fact that some real changes have occurred in the status of women (or of African Americans and Afro-Caribbeans) over the century. Along similar lines, Walby has made the point that "many policy demands that were once considered radical and feminist are no longer described as feminist" (1997, 163).

There are of course many other possible examples of change, all with different (and also diverse) connotations. From within the language and gender research tradition, many recent studies have examined the ways in which different groups of women (as with *queers* and *niggers*) have resisted existing power relations through linguistic strategies, successfully challenging hegemonic definitions and constructions (see, for example, Bucholtz 1996 and the chapters in the section titled Agency through Appropriation in Hall and Bucholtz 1995). At the same time, linguistic resistance can act as an active agent in the (re)construction of individual identity (e.g., Bucholtz, Liang, and Sutton 1999).

Language is fluid, and it both reflects and is implicated in changes in attitudes and behavior. Initially, perhaps, the identification of a specific discursive usage—and the provision of an alternative—may be a political action, undertaken by specific actors within specific social movements with specific goals. Linguistic strategies of resistance have included emphasizing gender neutrality, encouraging feminization (making women visible through gender specification), and adopting generic terms to replace the masculine (Curzan 2003). For example, there is a well-documented history of the movement in the United States in the 1970s toward gender-neutral language in scholarly and professional publications in the educational sphere. During this period, several major publishing houses, professional associations, and educational organizations developed and adopted guidelines on the nonsexist use of language (see, for example, Nilsen 1987). Another example is the resistance to national government definitions of ethnicity (e.g., the rejection in the 1960s in the United States of the classification *nonwhite* and the adoption of the term *Black* as a statement of identity by the Black power movement—Van Den Bergh 1987). But shifts in meaning are also constructed and made manifest in daily interaction and consequently enter into the complex space between discourse and action, where causation is inextricably intertwined with instantiation.

Within the sociological literature on changing family structures is an account of the relationship between changes in language, attitudes, and behavior that is particularly relevant to the line of argument I am putting forward. In this approach, which acknowledges a debt to Plummer's *Telling Sexual Stories* (1995), new stories or narrative forms help in the conceiving of new forms of family and intimate life. Thus new ways of linguistic expression indicate and instantiate both changing perceptions and changing possibilities of behavior (Weeks, Heaphy, and Donovan 1999). The process, operating at several different levels, is formulated thus:

> New stories about sexual and intimate life emerge . . . when there is a new audience ready to hear them in communities of meaning and understanding, and when new vocal groups can have their experiences validated in and through them. This in turn gives rise to new demands for recognition and validation as the new narratives circulate. These demands may be the expressions of a minority, but they resonate with broader changes in intimate life. (299)

This formulation is helpful in that it tries to deal analytically with the interaction between different levels (here, the narrative and "broader changes in intimate life"), and it may be that elements of it can usefully be generalized. Interestingly, the narratives approach comes from within the literature on masculinities. This is no coincidence, since the bulk of this literature has been directly concerned with issues of pluralities in, and changing symbolic representations of, masculinity. In the final section of this chapter, I turn to this aspect of the wider discursive environment with a focus on some examples from some of the by now relatively extensive literature on changing images of fatherhood and masculine caring behaviors.

Changing Masculinities and Fatherhood

The recent worldwide growth of research on changing symbolic representations of masculinities has been documented by Connell (2000). While the field experienced a massive burgeoning in the 1990s, even in the 1970s researchers noted an increase in images of "the new father," together with new expectations of involvement in parenting (discussed in Coltrane 1998). In the mid-1980s Lewis and Sussman, in a book titled *Men's Changing Roles in the Family*, already made the point that the gender research pendulum was swinging more in the direction of men, evidenced by "a birthquake of polemics, theorizing and research on changing men's roles with concentration on marital, family and parenting behaviors" (1986, xiv).

Writers on masculinity have been at the forefront of arguments both for the significance of changing images of masculinity and fatherhood and for the existence of real change in gender practice, particularly in relation to masculine caring behavior (e.g., Gerson 1993; Hood 1993; Coltrane 1996, 1998; Deutsch 1999). From this enormous literature I can give here only a very sketchy review, focusing on those aspects that are most significant for the central argument of this book. With respect to the question of changing images, this involves changes at the level of discourse, or symbolic representation, in particular the "new father" who is, according to Knijn (1995), becoming part of male gender identification. More recently, postmodernist writing on diversity and shifting meanings has generated a more complex perspective. For example, the "nurturant new father" referred to by Hochschild (1995) is "born in a context of multiplying ideals and images of a good father" (221). Here Hochschild argues for the existence of a wide diversity of choice of fathering styles in contradistinction to the simplistic media image of the new father. The point is taken further by Smart and Neale (1999) when they refer to the image of the new father as being composed of different and often contradictory elements. Likewise, the changing images associated with masculinity emerge from a context of plurality, in which, according to Connell (2000), there exists a hierarchy of masculinities, including a hegemonic masculinity and other subordinate forms that can provide alternative images, including versions containing elements usually associated with feminine caring behavior. In line with the emphasis on change, we should focus here on the links between discursive plurality, shifts in meaning, and changes in practice. The question in this context can be phrased thus: To what extent can the emergence of new and shifting images and ideals of fatherhood and masculinity be linked to empirical changes in practice?

Research from the 1980s documents some changes in paternal behavior, particularly the increase in paternal involvement in child care (Lewis

1986; Pleck, Lamb, and Levine 1986), but at the time, despite much media hype, there was little hard evidence in support of the claim for change in behavior (Lewis and Sussman 1986). However, at the turn of the twenty-first century more evidence is available (e.g., Bianchi's 2000 report that fathers are spending more time with their children than in the past), and there is now more general agreement in support of Coltrane's claim that "the move is towards uncoupling gender from caring" (1998, 106).

For instance, recent (and not so recent) studies show changes in masculine behavior associated with the taking on of routine responsibility for child care (see, for example, Coltrane 1996)—the quantitative changes in time use detailed in the following chapter support this position. In addition, a growing body of research focuses on "involved" fathers or even equal caretakers—fathers who participate to greater degrees in caring for children, as opposed to assuming the traditional breadwinner role. Typically, involved fathers do not make a distinction between mothering and fathering in caring (Gerson 2001). A number of authors have directly addressed the theoretical issue of the reasons for such changes in the meaning and practice of fatherhood. Beck and Beck-Gernsheim (1995) combine an argument about the social forces of late modernity generating increasing individualization, autonomy, and divorce from family ties with the growing significance of the parent-child bond as an enduring element in the face of increasing divorce rates. However, other authors place more emphasis on the issues of personal identity (e.g., Giddens 1992; Knijn 1995), arguing that increases in involved fatherhood are "in line with the growing awareness of, or belief in, personal identity as a reflexive identity" (Knijn, 16). I return to this issue of personal identity and its significance later in the book, when I discuss changes in intimacy and gender consciousness.

Once again, some of the more optimistic prognoses of future change should probably be regarded with caution; it may be the case that new ideals of fatherhood, currently manifested mostly among the middle classes, will be more likely to spread in the future (Lamb 1986). Indeed, some evidence suggests that class differences are changing in this respect—Gerson's (2001) study of involved fathers shows no differences between classes, although the sample was small. In chapter 5, I present findings that suggest a narrowing of the class difference in male partners' contribution to the domestic division of labor from a series of large-scale studies in Britain. But against this more optimistic vision we should set a variety of arguments, ranging from the practical to the theoretical. On the practical side, and remaining relatively positive, we can cite the difficulties faced by those men who do try to respond to changing images of fatherhood, who frequently encounter the same dilemmas faced by mothers with careers (Gerson 2001). But the more significant question here may be, what about absent fatherhood? The evidence on changing family structures shows an increasing countertrend toward single motherhood throughout Europe and North America. Among certain groups of the population, notably African Americans in the United States, the percentage of children living with their mother alone has for some time exceeded the percentage living together with both biological parents. Nonresidential fathers in the United States tend to live significant distances away from their children, and levels of contact are rated as intermediate (Acock and Demo 1994). Clearly, fatherhood itself is in these cases either a nonexistent or a severely attenuated role.

In addition, there is still resistance to the idea that progressive change in this area is even a possibility. The reasons for this resistance are both political, connected to the backlash against feminism, and theoretical. It is easier to dismiss the backlash arguments, which are largely based on an essentialized vision of masculinity and femininity. For example, Dench writes that the message of change "fails to recognize differences between men and women which have implications for the successful organization of family life" (1999, xii) and that "as we move into the new millennium we can expect a steady return to normalcy [sic] in family and sexual relations" (42).

These assertions are clearly based on essentialized assumptions about the normal roles for men and women, where "normal" is heavily laden with both its normative connotations of (biologically) right and inevitable. However, other more theoretically grounded positions are antithetical to the idea of change in gender relations and deserve more of our attention. For example, Risman hints at the materialist argument about the interest of men when she asks the rhetorical question, "Can men mother?" She answers that they can, but in most traditional marriages they don't have to. The fact is that women will do it for them, and, crucially, everyone believes that this is what should happen (Risman 1998). Here men's expectations of what women should provide for them, and, not entirely symmetrically, women's expectations of what they should provide for men, clearly go much deeper than the simply materialist. But the materialist argument appears explicitly in the approach of McMahon (1999), who presents men as the "agents" of the stalled revolution. In an analysis focused on public discourse around the issue of men's change, McMahon argues that it is in men's interest to remain the dominant group, and therefore the prospects for change are bleak. It should be said, I think, that among serious authors in the field of masculinities, this devotion to the "no change" argument is relatively rare. It shares more in common theoretically with an earlier period of resistance to the idea of change among researchers in the area of the domestic division of labor, which I discussed in chapter 2.

Summary and Conclusion

To summarize this brief review of evidence for change in the wider discursive context, the overall picture suggests shifts in attitudes, language, and symbolic representations occurring both within and between successive generations and interplaying with slow changes in other practices, such as changes in fatherhood behaviors. In part III of this book I discuss the emergence of new ideals of intimate relationships. If (as appears to be the case) these ideals coexist with changes in attitudes and language representation that move in the same direction, then this further strengthens the case for change in the discursive environment. But before I move on to develop a framework based on these ideas, in the following chapters I complete this review of the multilayered evidence for change by presenting some quantitative empirical evidence for change in behavior relating to the domestic division of labor. As I have suggested, it is the *coincidence* of changes in the wider discursive context, such as those discussed in this chapter, with the growing empirical evidence for changes in gender practices in the home that deserves our serious attention.

CROSS-NATIONAL TRENDS IN DOMESTIC LABOR PRACTICES: CONVERGENCE OVER TIME?

) (

In this chapter, and the one following, I turn to a different level of evidence in the multilayered picture I am presenting. Whereas the previous chapter addresses evidence for change in elements of the wider discursive context, in this chapter I present multinational quantitative empirical evidence for change in practices in the home relating to the domestic division of labor. Based on large-scale nationally representative data sets, this evidence stretches in time from the 1960s to the 1990s. But the importance of the quantitative evidence to the argument about change is related not only to its scale. It is also a question of consistency: Quantitative analyses of consistent measures across time can actually measure change. Studies that focus on single points in time are rarely directly comparable, and evidence that focuses on changing discourses is of a different order altogether. But the significant point is the correlation of the direction of the different levels of evidence for change, including both the discursive and the quantitative.

Time-Use Diary Method and Evidence

Several sources provide quantitative evidence for long-term changes over time in the allocation of household labor. The most reliable are based on successive surveys with comparable measures or on longitudinal data, such as the NSFH panel (e.g., Gupta 1999). However, time-use diary studies are by now perhaps the main source of large-scale empirical evidence in this area, and many recent texts based on this approach have referred to the growing evidence for change in the division of domestic labor (e.g., Niemi 1995; Robinson and Godbey 1997; Crompton and Harris 1999; Gershuny 2000). *Within* specific countries there have been changes in the amount of time that men and women spend in housework in the direction of greater equity (see Gershuny 2000 for Britain; Robinson and Godbey 1997 for the United States).

Time-use data are derived from diary surveys in which respondents record their activities throughout the day as a sequence of coded digits representing different activities. Such data have provided important information about the pattern of activities of individuals, households, and societies. At the macrolevel, estimates can be derived of how time is divided between production and consumption activities within a society (Gershuny 2000), while at the microlevel information is provided about how individuals divide their time between paid and unpaid work or the amount and use of leisure time (Gershuny and Sullivan 1998).

So what makes this particular form of evidence both interesting and reliable in the current context? Why might relative changes in the time spent in household work by men and women be considered important, and why would we rely on time-use diary studies to provide this information? The answers to these questions are both theoretical and methodological. First, we need to distinguish between various definitions of time (although a full discussion of the literature is beyond the scope of this book). *Historical* time is one of the critical elements in any consideration of the pace and extent of change, since change necessarily implies time. One of the questions that underlie the focus of this book is, how much historical time is needed for a change in gender practices to be manifest? On the other hand, considerations of *individual* time and how it is distributed are significant in determining the patterns of change. Walby has said that time represents "a key to the understanding of change and diversity in gender roles" and plays a role as an "active resource in the creation of [this] change" (1997, 8).

In considering individual time, both clock time (as measured for example in time-use diaries) and perceived time, in which time is socially constructed and refracted by individuals (see Adam 1995), have been seen as important measures. The distinction is based on the assertion that two types of essentially opposed time exist: natural time (clock time) and social time (perceived time). E. P. Thompson (1965) is generally referenced as the source of this distinction, although his original description has been somewhat modified. Based on this dualistic conception, the kind of time measured by the time-use diary has been criticized as linear, coldly statistical, and devoid of human meaning. However, the idea of two competing types of temporality, one scientific or statistical and one social, is questionable (see Gershuny and Sullivan 1998 for a fuller discussion and defense of the methodology). There is a distinguished literature on the simultaneous coexistence of different notions of time within the same societies, including references within Thompson's seminal work. The theme is perhaps best summarized by Le Goff: "At the heart of the same society, of the same ideology, there can and must coexist different times, a multiplicity and plurality of times" (1981, 116) (my translation[1]).

It is undeniably the case that one aspect of the human experience of time in industrialized societies subject to clock time is precisely that of a linear sequence or progression of activities. The argument as expressed in Gershuny and Sullivan (1998) in support of time-use diary research is thus that one way of appropriately measuring time is to measure the duration and density of the activities that constitute those sequences. In this chapter I focus on the large-scale evidence for changes in the use of time by individuals, specifically on the changes evident in domestic time use by women and men in their day-to-day lives, both over time and cross-culturally.

The second reason for the growth of interest in time-use studies in this area is methodological. I devote attention to this issue since the methodology is still not without its detractors. Time-use data collected in the form of standardized diaries have for many years provided us with information on the pattern of daily activities. These data can be analyzed to provide estimates of total work time (paid and unpaid), the division of domestic labor, and the amount and use of leisure time. Diary keeping is a well-tried research collection methodology yielding descriptions that are rooted in routine everyday experience, and as noted already, time-use diary studies are by now perhaps the main source of evidence for changes over time in the domestic division of labor between men and women.

Diary estimates of the time spent in different domestic activities, where people record their participation in those activities with at least some degree of contemporaneity, differ from estimates based on responses to such questions in surveys. It can safely be assumed that diary estimates are in fact the more accurate since they do not involve the problems of retrospective recall and since it is much harder to "cheat" in order to achieve a certain overall proportion of time spent in a particular activity (see Juster 1985; Robinson 1985; Kalfs 1993). The notorious example of husbands' and wives' differing accounts from interview data of the proportion of domestic work undertaken by the husband illustrates this point—the husband's estimate is routinely greater than that of the wife (see Edgell 1980; Berk 1985; Bittman and Lovejoy 1993).

On the other hand, it has been argued that since diary keeping constitutes a relatively time-consuming and strenuous activity in itself, nonresponse rates will tend to render it relatively useless. While this criticism may have been rightfully applied to the earliest time-use diary surveys (which date from the 1920s), more recent developments in the design of diary instruments and surveys have rendered it outdated (Robinson and Converse 1972). In addition, "bad" diarists are not readily identifiable according to conventional sociodemographic indicators (Gershuny 1990, 1995)—which indicates that biases introduced by nonresponse are not strongly related to the commonly used explanatory variables of social research. A final frequent criticism of diary data is that the act of diary keeping is itself likely to lead to alterations in behavior. While this may be a strong argument in relation to the recording of specific behaviors (e.g., alcohol intake or calorie consumption), it is much less clear that it applies to the continual recording of daily activities required by a time-use diary, where no particular activity is emphasized. These and other methodological criticisms have already been extensively documented and convincingly refuted in several sources (e.g., Robinson 1985; Dow and Juster 1985; Kalfs 1993). So although time-use diaries have been criticized in the past as a methodology, their importance is now increasingly recognized as a means of ascertaining changes in practice in a more valid and reliable way than one-off survey questions on behavior.

The main challenge to the validity of time-use diary evidence, particularly in the area of the division of domestic labor, has recently undergone something of a shift of emphasis, away from a direct questioning of its accuracy in describing change (e.g., Hochschild 1989) toward a discussion of whether we can talk about the kind of changes described as meaningful. In addition to the question of whether clock time can provide an appropriately meaningful measure of human experience, we can cite here the argument already referred to in a previous chapter that quantifiable change in the time spent by men on specific domestic tasks does not constitute real change in the distribution of *responsibility for* or *management of* those tasks (e.g., Pahl 1989; Jamieson 1999). As noted before, this is an important consideration, and I return to it later in the chapter. However, at the same time, it is now widely accepted that some changes in the direction of greater gender equality have occurred, at least in the *fulfillment* of domestic tasks. This acceptance in itself represents a shift in perspective in the literature over the past decades. I now turn to long-term trends in the overall average amounts of time that men and women spend in domestic work.

Changing Patterns of Time Use: A Cross-National Analysis

Various authors have analyzed changing patterns of time use in single countries using time-use diary data and arrived at similar conclusions (notably Robinson and Godbey in the United States, 1997; Bittman in Australia, 1998; and Gershuny and Jones in Britain, 1987). Evidence from all these countries indicates an increase for men from the 1960s through to the 1990s in the time spent in unpaid domestic work. At the same time, women's domestic work hours on average decreased (from a much higher base of course), so the overall effect is of a trend toward convergence in the distribution for men and women over time. For example, Robinson and Godbey documented an increase in men's domestic work (including housework and child care) in the United States of 4.2 hours per week from 1965 to 1985 and a decrease of 9.3 hours for women. Analyses extending the time period to 1995 suggest that the same trends have continued for both men and women (Gershuny 2000).

In Australia, men's unpaid work increased by 3.6 hours a week between 1974 and 1992, compared with a decrease for women of 6.5 hours (Bittman 1998). In Britain, overall domestic work undertaken by men increased by 3.6 hours a week from 1961 to 1984 (Gershuny and Jones 1987), while a more recent analysis shows that the period 1985 to 1999 saw an overall increase of 1.3 hours a week in men's participation in core domestic work (cooking, cleaning, and clothes care) compared with a decrease for women of 3 hours a week, while taking into account household structure and employment status (Gershuny 2000). These kinds of changes are by now widely reported. That they are also meaningful can be argued from the fact that they are comparable in magnitude to the average decrease in paid work hours for full-time employees in many Western societies over the past thirty years, a trend that is widely referred to in discussion of changing employment structures (e.g., Crouch and Streeck 1997).

Some of the most up-to-date cross-national comparative research on changes in the use of time is based on the multinational time-use data archive held at the University of Essex, England. The large-scale nationally representative surveys of the archive cover the 1960s through to the year 2000 for more than twenty countries in North America and Europe. Some countries are represented by only a single survey, but most are now represented by two or three surveys (up to five) over this period (see Gershuny 2000). The cross-national analyses reported here are based on a subset of countries from northern Europe and North America, which were selected on the basis of their data continuity and quality (the specific surveys used are shown in table 4.1a). The last column of table 4.1b shows

Table 4.1. Time-Use Diary Survey Dates and Number of Cases

(a) Survey Dates

	1961–1971	1972–1981	1982–1995
Canada	1971	1981	1986; 1992
Finland		1979	1987
Netherlands		1975; 1980	1985
Norway	1971	1981	
United Kingdom	1961	1975	1985; 1995
United States	1965	1975	1985

(b) Number of Cases

	Unweighted Cases			
	1961–1971	1972–1981	1982–1995	Total
Canada	1,828	1,845	8,138	11,811
Finland		8,309	10,277	18,586
Netherlands		3,121	2,348	5,469
Norway	4,309	3,410		7,719
United Kingdom	1,702	1,901	1,996	5,599
United States	1,790	1,753	2,268	5,811
Total	9,629	20,339	25,027	54,995

the total number of cases. Although they are all large in terms of sample numbers, the surveys from the different countries are of rather different sizes (having in total, for example, more than three times as many cases in Finland as in the Netherlands). Accordingly the cases have been weighted to give the same representation to each country in the aggregated data set: The weighted samples are representative of the respective national populations aged twenty to fifty-nine at the time of the survey.[2]

To analyze change in time-use patterns, it is necessary to make a distinction between the particular change that is of direct relevance to the research and the related compositional changes in the population, so as to take account of the latter by holding them constant in analysis. For example, one question that is frequently raised in relation to changes in the proportion of time that men and women devote to domestic labor relates to changes in women's participation in the paid labor market. Between 1960 and 2000 there has been a considerable rise in the proportion of women in employment in the major industrialized countries. All other things being equal, this would be reflected in a rising trend toward overall changes in the amount of women's time devoted to employment, along with corresponding reductions in other areas, such as leisure or unpaid work. Similarly, the use of time is also strongly dependent on family status (e.g., mothers of young children are less likely to be in full-time employment and more likely to be spending more time in unpaid domestic labor). Therefore changes in the composition of families over time will also have an effect at the overall level on the amount of time devoted to both paid and unpaid labor.

But of interest in these analyses is whether we can detect changes in the use of time that are not *directly* the result of structural adjustments to changes in female employment or changes in the composition of families (although these factors may have important indirect effects). It is possible in analysis to distinguish such changes if the relevant structural changes can be identified and held constant (controlled for). We are trying to find the same sorts of changes going on *within* the different structural subgroups over time (e.g., for both employed and nonemployed women or for families both with and without young children). These analyses were therefore designed to show the effect of changes over time in broad categories of time use when holding constant the effects of family status and employment status for each survey. The variables entered into the analysis were family status, employment status and country (as controls for structural variation), and historical time period (to show the trend over time).

For the sake of clarity and accessibility, I have chosen to present graphs of the analyses that show ordinary least squares regression lines for the changes over time in unpaid work time while holding constant the effects of family status and employment status for each survey. Also held constant are the interaction effects between family status and time and between employment status and time (the interaction effects with time are those that control for compositional changes in family status and employment status over time). More statistically elaborate versions of the analyses on which these graphs are based may be found in Sullivan and Gershuny 2001 and Gershuny 2000—the conclusions are the same.[3]

The figures show trends in minutes per day devoted to specific activities for women and men in full-time employment with children between the ages of five and fifteen living in the same household. These groups were chosen to illustrate the nature of change in men's and women's time on a comparable basis (the comparison of men and women who are full-time employees is a common strategy in research where the question of equity in housework is the issue). Where there exist important differentials between these groups and those in other employment and family statuses, I refer in the text to the effect of being in these different statuses (e.g., trends in unpaid work for women employed part time with children under five in the household are discussed later in the chapter).

Taking all unpaid work together (including routine domestic work such as cooking, cleaning, and clothes care; shopping; traveling; doing odd jobs; and caring for children), figures 4.1 and 4.2 show a substantial differential in trends by sex. There is little evidence for change in the amount of time women spend in these activities, with most of the trends for different countries being relatively weak and going in opposite directions (see figure 4.1). A slight overall upward trend is just statistically significant ($p < .05$). In contrast, the graph for men's overall unpaid work time (figure 4.2) shows a pronounced upward trend for all countries analyzed from a much lower initial level, amounting to an increase of more than 20 minutes during the time covered by the analyses. This increase is highly statistically significant ($p < .001$).

The two figures are shown on the same scale to emphasize the different levels for men and women (remember that these women and men are

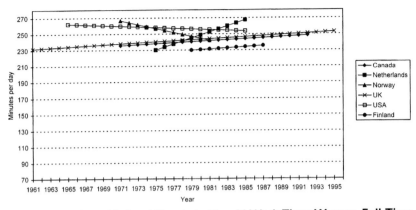

Figure 4.1. Cross-National Trends in Unpaid Work Time: Women, Full-Time Employed with Children Aged Five to Fifteen in the Household

in the same employment and family status categories!). Referring to the figures, it is possible to get some idea of these different levels in terms of absolute amounts of time spent in unpaid labor. From figure 4.1 it is clear that, at the approximate overall average level, the amount of time contributed by women to unpaid domestic labor over the period did not change that much, staying at around 250 minutes (more than four hours per day). In contrast, the graph for men shows an increase in the overall average, which rises from a level somewhere above 100 minutes per day during the 1960s to somewhere below 150 minutes by the 1990s. Thinking

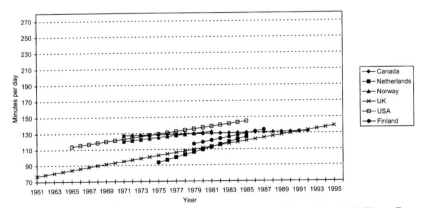

Figure 4.2. Cross-National Trends in Unpaid Work Time: Men, Full-Time Employed with Children Aged Five to Fifteen in the Household

about these numbers in proportional terms, men's overall contribution increased from less than one-third of that of women in the earlier period to over one-third in the 1990s. Remember that these estimates apply to full-time employed women and men with children aged five to fifteen in the household. Given that full-time employed women do less unpaid work than do other women, and that the husbands of such women do relatively more than other (married) men (from the literature on differences by type of household; see chapter 5), it can be assumed that this represents an underestimate of the average amount of time that *all* women spend in unpaid labor and an overestimate of the average contribution of all men. However, as I have said, although the *levels* might be different for different groups, the *relative changes* for men and women do not vary substantially between the different groups over time.

Figures 4.1 and 4.2 show changes in the overall category of unpaid labor. However, this category is composed of several different components, which we know from previous research are distinct in terms of their relationship to gendered practices in the home. So in order to delve deeper, the unpaid work classification used for figures 4.1 and 4.2 can be broken down into the three elements: routine domestic work, shopping and travel, and child care. This division enables direct comparison with the findings of Robinson and Godbey (1997) and Bittman (1998) with respect to routine domestic work in the United States and Australia (discussed previously). It also enables a contribution to other debates concerning, for example, the question of changes in the time devoted to child care by parents, both of whom are in full-time employment.

Taking core domestic work time (i.e., cooking, cleaning, and clothes care) first, a steep decline is evident in the time women spend in these activities, amounting to an hour a day (figure 4.3). This trend is highly statistically significant ($p < .001$).[4] Once again, a consistent increase is evident in men's participation across all countries analyzed (see figure 4.4). This increase of 18 minutes per day over the time period is also highly statistically significant ($p < .001$).

These findings are consistent with others reported in the literature based on diary data, having been noted recently by Gershuny, Godwin, and Jones (1994), Niemi (1995), Robinson and Godbey (1997), and Bittman (1998) among others. However, in general discussions of the di-

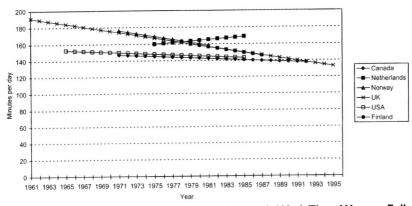

Figure 4.3. Cross-National Trends in Core Domestic Work Time: Women, Full-Time Employed with Children Aged Five to Fifteen in the Household

vision of domestic labor more attention has, perhaps rightly, been given to the continuing disparity of performance of these tasks by men and women, even when both are in full-time employment (as in the analyses shown here). Figures 4.1 and 4.2 have already illustrated the continuing gap between the sexes in this area. My point here is that there is evidence for some convergence, as indicated by the downward trend for women in the core categories of housework (cooking, cleaning, clothes care), taken together with the upward trend for men. If we roughly gauge the overall levels from the figures again, we can see a decrease in core domestic work

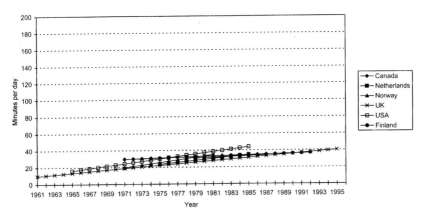

Figure 4.4. Cross-National Trends in Core Domestic Work Time: Men, Full-Time Employed with Children Aged Five to Fifteen in the Household

for women from something around 175 minutes per day (nearly three hours) in the earlier period to something less than 140 minutes per day in the 1990s. The *increase* for men is in relative terms more dramatic, but from a much lower base—around 20 minutes a day in the earlier period to about 40 minutes a day in the 1990s. The rough proportional change in men's overall contribution shown in these figures is therefore from less than 15 percent in the earlier period to nearly 25 percent in the 1990s.

The increase in men's participation in core domestic activities is consistent with the overall increase in men's unpaid work time. But for women, while the time trend for core domestic work is strongly negative, there was a slight *increase* in overall unpaid work (see figure 4.1). The answer to this apparent contradiction lies in the trends for the other two main elements of unpaid work: (1) shopping and travel and (2) child care, both of which have increased markedly and consistently over this time period for women (as well as for men). Although previous studies based on time-use data have shown the decline in core domestic work for women and the increase for men, the increase in these other elements of unpaid labor has not been widely reported.

Figures 4.5 and 4.6 show the increase in time spent in shopping and travel activities since the 1960s for women and men respectively.

For both sexes the increase is statistically significant ($p < .05$). It is perhaps surprising that this finding has not received more attention, since the trends that have led to it are well known: an increase over the period

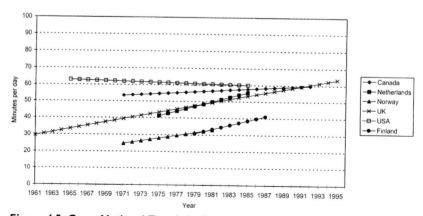

Figure 4.5. Cross-National Trends in Shopping and Travel Time: Women, Full-Time Employed with Children Aged Five to Fifteen in the Household

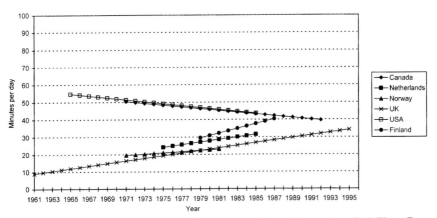

Figure 4.6. Cross-National Trends in Shopping and Travel Time: Men, Full-Time Employed with Children Aged Five to Fifteen in the Household

covered by the analysis both in the possession of and in the use of cars for shopping, for leisure activities, and for ferrying children.[5] In addition, the increasing externalization of costs by businesses (e.g., the growing propensity to locate on cheaper out-of-town sites in shopping malls) means that the time spent both traveling and shopping has risen. Both women's and men's time spent in these activities has increased, suggesting that there are behavioral differences between changes in these elements of unpaid work (which were in any case always distributed somewhat more equally between men and women) and those of the routine (and routinely gendered) domestic tasks such as cooking, cleaning, and clothes care.

The same point can be made for child-care activities. The amount of time devoted to this aspect of unpaid work has also increased for full-time employed women and, less strongly, for men (see figures 4.7 and 4.8; trends significant at $p < .001$ and $p < .01$, respectively). This increase supports Robinson and Godbey's (1997) conclusion from U.S. data that the time spent in child care has increased for women (men were not reported on). Again, this result has been observed before from time-use diary data (see Gershuny 1990), but its implications in respect to other research, in this case on parenting and child care, have not been addressed to any great extent until very recently (although Bianchi reported in 2000 that mothers' time with children has been quite stable over time). What needs emphasizing here is that the empirical observation of increasing (or even stable) amounts of time devoted to child care runs entirely contrary

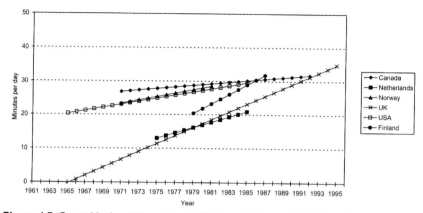

Figure 4.7. Cross-National Trends in Child Care: Women, Full-Time Employed with Children Aged Five to Fifteen in the Household

to current concerns about the neglect of children, evident both in the media and in much-quoted academic works such as that of Hewlett (1991, emotively titled *When the Bough Breaks*).

Various arguments might be made to explain increases in child-care time without contradicting the idea that children receive less of our attention. The most obvious of these—that there are more children in families—is clearly not borne out by information on fertility rates and household structures. There is also little evidence for a decline in the substitution of other relatives in child care; in fact the increased numbers of grandparents

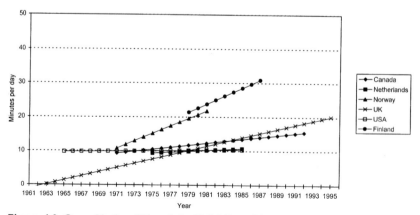

Figure 4.8. Cross-National Trends in Child Care: Men, Full-Time Employed with Children Aged Five to Fifteen in the Household

would suggest at least the existence of a wider potential pool of support. Some evidence is now beginning to emerge for the significance of this source of support. Likewise, little is known about the comparative relative costs of child-care providers (e.g., day care, babysitters, nannies) since a substantial part of that market is unlicensed. In any event, what we observe from the analyses is an increase in the time devoted to child care at a population level, which is consistent between countries with different policies and regulations on child care.

Bianchi suggests that employed mothers seek ways to maximize time with their children by cutting down on other activities such as housework and voluntary work. This is in line with changes in the meaning and nature of child care, involving a growing emphasis on participation in child-related activities. For example, parents participating actively in their children's homework was certainly more characteristic of the 1990s than it was of the 1960s. Consistent with this is the argument that at least part of the trend observed in figures 4.7 and 4.8 can be accounted for by changes in the recording of activities, relating to whether activities are perceived by respondents as child centered or not. For example, note the very low levels of reporting of child-care activities in 1961 in the United Kingdom. Clearly, in the 1960s parents would have spent *some* time in various activities in the company of their children. Equally, part of the strongly upward trend from that point would certainly reflect a real growth in child-related activities. However, there is also likely to be a reporting effect at work here, reflecting perhaps an increased sensitivity among parents to the significance of time spent with children. In the earlier decades, activities involving children were likely to have been reported in the diary by reference to the activity itself (e.g., "went to football—with children"), whereas a more recent diary might more consciously record "took children to football." The former activity is more likely to be classified as "attendance at sporting event," whereas the latter might perhaps be properly referred to as a "child-care-related activity." But the implied change in the reporting of these activities suggests real changes in the salience of child care over the last three decades.

It should be emphasized that while the *levels* of unpaid work (in terms of the amount of time contributed) vary by different family and employment statuses in accordance with previous work (see chapter 5 on differences), the time *trends* shown here do not vary substantively. This means that, although the figures reflect men and women in a particular combination of employment and family status (full-time employed, with children between five and fifteen in the household), the resulting trends for unpaid work are not substantially altered by the choice of a different reference group. For example, if women in part-time employment with children under five in the household are selected, the conclusions for the various combinations of unpaid work remain the same (i.e., a slight overall increase in unpaid work, accounted for by a decrease in core domestic tasks accompanied by an increase in the time spent in both shopping and child care). For this particular group, however, there *is* one important difference in the findings for overall work (i.e., both paid and unpaid work) and leisure time. While there was a statistically significant *decrease* in overall work time for women in full-time employment with older children in the household, there was no change in the overall work time for part-time employed women with small children (Sullivan and Gershuny 2001). Women in this category are likely to be under the greatest time pressure, through having to combine child care with a job. The decrease in paid work time for this group is balanced by a stronger increase in unpaid work, composed of increases in the time spent in shopping, traveling, and child care. The result is no overall increase in leisure time for this particularly pressured group.

Summary and Conclusion

Large-scale empirical data provide a different layer of the multilayered picture to that presented in the previous chapter. In this chapter I present quantitative analyses of changes in the time spent by women and men on various unpaid labor tasks based on multinational time-use data from the 1960s through the 1990s. While the time that women devote every day to core domestic labor (cooking, cleaning, and clothes care) has decreased by just under an hour over the period, there has been an increase of around 20 minutes per day in the time men devote to these activities. These findings lend support to previous analyses in the literature showing changes in men's and women's time use for single countries.

In addition, these analyses have held constant the changes over time in both employment status and family status, as well as individual country effects. For example, in the case of employment status, the implication is that the increase in women's entry into paid employment over the period does not account for the reduction we observe in their domestic labor time, since we observe the same changes among women with different employment statuses.

One aspect of change that was not addressed directly in these analyses relates to the overall distribution of work and leisure for men and women over time. For if it can be shown that the increased contribution of men to unpaid work has been at the expense of their leisure time, this could perhaps be conceptualized as a more meaningful or important change than if a simple substitution of work times (unpaid for paid) was involved. A multivariate analysis of the same data source, in which a similar set of variables was held constant (i.e., family status, employment status, country, and historical time period), showed that while the time spent by men in paid work declined substantially, there was also a significant (although lesser) decrease in the time spent by men in leisure activities. So the average picture in terms of changes between the 1960s and the 1990s across the different categories of paid work, unpaid work, and leisure shows that while both paid work time and leisure time declined for men, their unpaid work time increased by an amount that was equivalent in magnitude to the combined decrease. For women, in contrast, there was a lesser, although still significant, increase in paid work time, a decrease in unpaid work time, and an *increase* in leisure time (Sullivan and Gershuny 2001, table II). In proportional terms, the decrease in leisure time for men accounted for about one-third of the increase in their time devoted to unpaid work—an indication that some substitution of leisure time for unpaid work time had taken place for men. So at the overall level at least (because one cannot assume directly from data at the macrolevel that these processes are the same within individual households), this substitution has contributed both to the reduction in unpaid work time for women and to an increase in their leisure time.

To return finally to the question of how much change means change and over how long, the overall increase in men's contribution to core domestic work may not seem that impressive if we calculate the decade changes (about 20 minutes over thirty years). In addition, it is still reasonable to emphasize the ongoing discrepancy between the overall amount of time that women and men spend in domestic work tasks. However, some authors (e.g., McMahon 1999) continue to argue that the main effect involved in any change is that of women's reduction in housework hours. As I discussed already, *both* the upward trend for men and the downward trend for women in the core domestic work tasks are consistent in direction across different countries and statistically significant when controlling for other relevant variables. That the trends for men and women move in opposing directions is also an important feature in the adjudication of a hypothesis for slow change at the overall level toward a situation of greater gender equality in the performance of domestic tasks.

While it is undeniable that, in terms of year-on-year differences, the magnitude of these changes appears small, especially for men, the trends involved are both statistically robust and consistent, both internally (i.e., over time and space) and externally (in relation to other evidence for change). And although statistical significance in itself does not mean a result is substantively important, the magnitude of the overall trend is, as I have said, comparable to that of the average decrease in paid work time for full-time employees evident in many Western industrialized societies over the past thirty years, a change that is widely acknowledged and deemed meaningful (e.g., Crouch and Streeck 1997). Thus, we must conclude that, on the basis of time spent in these tasks (with all the inadequacies of this measure in relation to the content of that time), a substantial reduction in gender inequality in the performance of some of the normatively feminine-associated tasks within households appears to have taken place.

Having said all this, particular kinds of domestic work tasks remain strongly gendered. The question remains whether meaningful change is compatible with an ongoing gender-specific pattern of domestic task performance and management. Perhaps it is necessary to distinguish between a gender-specific *pattern* of domestic task performance and the gendering of domestic tasks as a *process* in the creation and maintenance of the "gender structure" (Risman 1998, 2004). Conceptualized in these terms, we can ask the following empirical question: Might it be possible to observe changes in the former before (or even without) changes in the latter? Proponents of the "no meaningful change" argument claim that the changes described in time-use analyses are both small and insignificant. I argue the reverse. First, the increase in men's participation in domestic work as reflected in time-use diaries is as substantial as changes in paid work times. Second, the point is really the *weight* of the evidence for many different kinds of change occurring simultaneously.

One important part of the empirical evidence on changing practice is missing from this chapter. The analyses presented here were all conducted at the aggregate level—in order to make the point about trends—and consequently they have ignored the question of differences in change between individuals and groups. However, recent research, particularly that influenced by poststructuralist feminist analysis, has pointed to the importance not just of documenting change at the average level but also of focusing on *differences* as a critical element of understanding. If we observe diversity between subgroups, what can this tell us about change? In the following chapter I discuss the issue of differences between groups of the population and present empirical evidence on *changing differences*.

Notes

1. «Au sein d'une même société, d'une même idéologie, peuvent et doivent co-exister des temps divers, une multiplicité, une pluralité de temps»

2. One statistical consequence of this weighting procedure is that the reported significance estimates are conservative.

3. Tables showing regression coeffients from the multinational, multivariate analysis can be found in the appendix; these tables were published in Sullivan and Gershuny (2001).

4. The countertrend of the Netherlands during this period is familiar from other research and has not been fully explained.

5. The distinction evident in figures 4.5 and 4.6 between Europe and North America may reflect a "catching up" effect for Europe following the earlier development of these trends in North America.

DIFFERENCE AND CHANGE IN DOMESTIC LABOR BETWEEN COUPLES: SOME MORE EQUAL THAN OTHERS?

) (

The current climate within gender theory puts a strong emphasis on diversity and difference as important components of a better theoretical understanding of social phenomena related to gender. So while the previous chapter describes large-scale changes in men's and women's contribution to various unpaid work tasks over a thirty-year period, focusing on the general overall trend, in this chapter I move to consider diversity between households. In particular I want to address the issue of difference *as related* to change.

I raise this issue because a vast majority of the studies of diversity between households in the area of domestic labor have made cross-sectional comparisons between subgroups of the population (e.g., employed versus unemployed, better educated versus less well educated, cohabiting versus married, African Americans versus Caucasian Americans, and so on) at the same period of time, presenting a static picture of stable differences. However, in order to explain change in this context, we must engage with the issue of the *interaction* between change and difference. Indeed, Marx Ferree (1991), on the basis of literature documenting various degrees of flexibility in the allocation of household work, suggests that a processual approach incorporating the idea of change can arise only in the context of a focus on plurality and difference among households. Only by close attention to diversity between households can we begin to understand the conditions under which it might be possible for change to occur. Here, in keeping with an emphasis on both diversity *and* change, I present some findings in this chapter on *changing differences* over time in partners' contribution to domestic labor. The idea of changing differences emphasizes the importance not only of cross-sectional connections between domestic labor practices and specific socioeconomic variables but also of the way these relationships have changed over time. This kind of analysis is made possible by the existence of successive time-use diary data sets as described in the previous chapter. Some countries, in particular Britain, have by now an impressive collection of such data sets, stretching from the 1960s to the present.

Much household research on differences has been conducted based on education level of partners, employment status of couples, and different family structures. This long tradition of research according to conventional socioeconomic and demographic indicators can be traced back to Vanek (1974), Oakley (1974), and beyond. More recently, researchers have also investigated couples from diverse ethnic groups and those with different sexual orientations. An article by Coltrane (2000), based on a review of the literature on family work published between 1989 and 1999, summarizes some of these empirical differences. In the analyses that follow, and based on the available data and variables, I have chosen a subset of socioeconomic and demographic variables to describe changing differences. These variables are all known to be significantly associated with domestic work practices, and it is on these that I focus for the remainder of the chapter. In doing so, I am aware that I am overlooking many other—perhaps equally important—indicators of difference. The analyses presented in this chapter can therefore be regarded as an example of an investigation of changing differences, which could (and should) be extended to other indicators of changing difference in future research.

Differences

In all the literature to date, one of the most consistent effects is found between the different categories of women's employment. Several issues come into play here: whether the woman is full time, part time, or not employed, as well as her earning power relative to her partner. When women are employed in full-time jobs, with high earning power relative to their partners, it appears that their male partners are likely to contribute more to domestic work. This finding has been most convincingly interpreted within the framework of a theory of marital power (e.g., Komter 1989; Pyke 1994), in which the earnings of men and women in a couple constitute resources in the balance of power between them, which in turn has consequences for how domestic labor is divided. In contrast to high-earning, full-time employed women, those women who are employed part time, and who have young children in the household, have the heaviest responsibilities and the smallest amount of leisure time.

Of the other main socioeconomic factors consistently found to be strongly associated with differences in the division of domestic labor, one of the strongest is the educational status of men. The higher the level of education, the more household work the man seems to do (both in absolute terms and relative to his female partner). Although conceptual difficulties arise with the interpretation of education level as a variable (Coltrane 2000), this effect has mainly been interpreted in terms of the differing values and ideologies of differently educated men (which may also reflect class differences). With respect to family status, there is convincing evidence that cohabiting couples have a more equitable domestic division of labor than do married couples (although a question mark still remains over whether this is due to structural differences between the two kinds of couples, such as the lower chance of there being children in the households of cohabiting couples). There is also some suggestion that those in second marriages share domestic tasks more equally. Again, various theories have been offered to explain this, including issues of experience in first marriages, selection of second partners, and the differing norms that apply to second marriages as opposed to first marriages (Cherlin 1978; Sullivan 1997a).

In short, explaining differences of these kinds between groups involves complex questions of relative power and differing ideologies, and, furthermore, the evidence is not always consistent. From a structuralist materialist position, emphasis is given to the additional power that women accrue in marriage from higher earnings, giving them greater command over the household resources needed to elicit cooperation from their partners. Others place greater importance on values (e.g., the greater commitment to egalitarianism associated with higher levels of education or within cohabitating couples). In any event it does appear that, irrespective of other variables, ideology can play an important independent role. One of the elements that Risman (1998) found among "fair" couples was equal earning power *in combination* with an egalitarian philosophy.

Changing Differences

These broad findings on diversity between the different categories of common sociodemographic and economic variables do not, however, address the relationship between difference and change. Within the conventional framework, change has tended to be thought of in terms of changes in the variables associated cross-sectionally with specific patterns of division of domestic labor. For example, since employed women on average tend to do relatively less household work than their nonemployed sisters, as more women move into employment the overall domestic division of labor will tend toward change in the direction of greater equality (see, for example, Baxter 1992). Or alternatively, changes in family status (in particular the presence of a young child in the household) may have a (temporary) impact on the way domestic labor is divided within the household, with male partners contributing more during these periods. Some evidence exists at the household level for the first of these changes, relating to employment. Research shows that the longer a woman in a couple relationship has spent in full-time employment, the more housework her partner is likely to do (Gershuny, Godwin, and Jones 1994). In addition, a move into full-time employment by the woman in a couple is likely to be followed by an adjustment in the domestic division of labor, with the man doing slightly more housework (and the woman substantially less). Gershuny, Godwin, and Jones pose the hypothesis of "lagged adaptation," suggesting there is a period of adjustment within couples to changes in women's employment during which no change in the division of housework is evident, followed by a movement in the direction of greater sharing (among those couples that stay together!). However, other authors, also reporting evidence for an increase in men's participation when their female partners are employed, conclude that changes in attitudes, rather than changes in family status variables, cause intergenerational change in men's participation (e.g., Goldscheider and Waite 1991).

Given the cross-sectional evidence for connections between a range of major socioeconomic variables and the domestic division of labor (and presuming always that the nature of these connections remains the same), an overall growth in more equal sharing patterns of domestic labor would be expected over time. This prediction arises from the connection between the domestic division of labor and level of education (rising), female employment (rising), and marriage patterns (with rising divorce and remarriage rates and later ages at marriage). However, missing from this macrolevel prognosis is an empirical documentation of difference and change, which can show the connection between some of these variables and how couples divide their domestic labor at different points in time. This would provide support for hypotheses about change arising from trends in these structural variables. But in addition, if it can be shown that the standard structural variables such as family status and employment status (and their combination) do not by themselves account for changes in practices around domestic labor, then the implication is that we need to look elsewhere for alternative sources of change—perhaps in the wider discursive environment.

A particularly good sequence of the sort of time-use diary data needed to provide evidence on structural differences and change in the division of domestic labor comes from Britain. Three time-use diary data sets for the years 1975, 1987, and 1997 were used in the analysis described here.[1] All were national-level studies, and couples defining themselves as married or living as married were selected from these data sets on the basis of age (male aged under sixty-six) and for being "good diarists."[2]

In chapter 4, the change in minutes per day spent by men and women in different domestic activities was used to chart trends over a range of industrialized countries. Since the analyses presented in this chapter are based on information from couples, rather than from individual men and women, it is possible here to show changes over time in the relative domestic division of labor between women and men *within* couples. So instead of just looking at macrolevel trends, we can focus on what is going on inside couples. The relative measure that tells us this is constructed by dividing the woman's (or the man's) contribution in terms of time by the total time spent in domestic tasks by both partners. This "relative domestic division of labor measure" shows how the overall burden of domestic work is divided *between partners*. I use it here to present changing differences over time in the connection between the domestic division of labor, employment status, and social class variables.

In addition, and in keeping with the emphasis on difference in this chapter, I also calculate another measure—one much less commonly seen. Since the focus here is on differences between households, as well as the overall relative domestic division of labor between men and women in couples, we might also want to assess change in the *percentage distribution* of couples according to their relative domestic division of labor. For example, is the subgroup in which women perform 90 percent or more of the domestic labor growing or shrinking in size over time relative to other subgroups? Or has there been a change in the percentage of couples with less traditionally gendered domestic divisions of labor (in which the woman contributes less than 60 percent, say, of the overall domestic work time) between 1975 and 1997? To answer these questions I introduce a second measure, in which the issue of "which couples change?" is analyzed in terms of trends in the percentage distribution of couples between subcategories of the relative domestic division of labor measure.

First, then, table 5.1 shows changing differences in the overall relative domestic division of labor measure for couples by survey year and employment status of partners. The table shows the proportion of couples' total domestic work time contributed by the woman.[3]

A clear decline can be seen in the average across all employment statuses from a level of 0.77 (i.e., the woman does 77 percent of the total domestic work of the couple) in 1975 to 0.63 (i.e., the woman does 63 percent of the total domestic work) in 1997. This represents a meaningful drop of 14 percentage points (or nearly one-fifth of the 1975 average). However, since it is already known from the literature on differences (see earlier in the chapter) that the domestic division of labor varies according to the employment status of partners, looking within the different combinations of employment status for men and women in couples shown in the

Table 5.1. Relative Division of Domestic Labor by Employment Status of Partners*

	1975	1987	1997	1975 N	1987 N	1997 N
All	0.77	0.67	0.63	680	388	175
Both full time	0.68	0.62	0.60	158	104	57
Husb ft, wife pt	0.80	0.70	0.69	199	120	34
Husb ft, wife ne	0.82	0.73	0.73	294	118	23
Other	0.61	0.55	0.59	29	46	61

*Among British couples of working age defining themselves as married or living as married
Key: Relative division of domestic labor measure = proportion of domestic work time contributed by women in couples; ft = full time; pt = part time; ne = not employed
Source: This table was originally published in Sullivan 2000.

table allows us to check whether this trend occurs across all employment status combinations. Here a number of features are notable. First, in accordance with what is already known from the literature, the woman's contribution to domestic work is highest when her partner is working full time and she is either nonemployed or working part time. This relationship holds true across the time span covered by the three surveys. The highest contribution by men is made in the residual category (Other), largely comprised of couples in which the man is either not employed or working only part time.[4] This confirms an observation made, among others, by Morris (1990), Wheelock (1990), and Orbuch and Eyster (1997) that (some) nonemployed men show a greater tendency to help around the house, although there is contradictory evidence from studies by Shelton and John (1993) and Brines (1994).

Second, although the change between 1987 and 1997 is less impressive than that between 1975 and 1987, it appears that the general declining trend observed in the overall average applies broadly across all the categories of couple employment status (with the exception of the small residual category, which shows a U-shaped pattern of change). This means that the average trend across all the employment status categories cannot be attributed to change in the division of domestic labor within any specific combination of employment statuses—for instance among full-time employed couples—but applies across all the major categories of couples' joint employment status. The other important implication is that change cannot simply be attributed to an increase in the proportion of women in full-time employment, since the same trend is in fact observable across the different combinations of couple employment status.

Table 5.2 shows the same relative measure by year of survey and couples' combined employment status, with the added dimension of household social class in the analysis. A distinction is made between two major class groups: manual/clerical and professional/technical.[5]

From table 5.2 it can be seen that the decline in women's contribution relative to men evident from table 5.1 applies equally to both major social class groups. In fact, the decline is considerably greater in magnitude than the difference between the social class categories at either date. If anything, there may be evidence for a larger increase in men's relative

Table 5.2. Relative Division of Domestic Labor by Employment Status of Partners and Socioeconomic Class of Household*

	Manual/Clerical		Professional/Technical	
	1975	1997	1975	1997
All	0.78	0.63	0.74	0.66
Both full time	0.69	0.60	0.62	0.62
Husb ft, wife pt	0.80	0.68	0.74	0.71
Husb ft, wife ne	0.82	0.73	0.80	0.73
Other	0.58	0.53	0.72	0.65

*Among British couples of working age defining themselves as married or living as married
Key: Relative division of domestic labor measure = proportion of domestic work time contributed by women in couples; ft = full time; pt = part time; ne = not employed
Source: This table was originally published in Sullivan 2000.

contribution (from a slightly lower base) among the manual and clerical category.

Again, looking across couples' combined employment status, evidence for an increase in men's relative contribution from 1975 through 1997 can be seen within most categories for both class groups, the only exception being for professional/technical couples where both are employed full time. However, this category recorded the most equal distribution of domestic labor in 1975 (at 62 percent contribution by the woman) and is surpassed in 1997 only by the manual/clerical group, where both members are employed full time (at a 60 percent contribution by the woman). Indeed, it may be suggested that the manual/clerical group in which both members of the couple are employed has eliminated, if not reversed, the class/gender gap in the division of domestic labor over the period between the surveys. In 1975, this group had relative domestic division of labor measures considerably higher than those for the professional/technical group of the same employment status (meaning that the women in the lower social class couples did relatively more). By 1997 this situation had equalized (even reversed?), with a *more* equal domestic division of labor among manual/clerical couples in employment than among their professional/technical equivalents.

It appears that over the twenty-two-year period between the surveys, manual/clerical couples in which both partners are employed had at the least caught up with the more equal distribution of domestic labor evident among equivalent professional/technical couples in 1975. This surprising development has not been recorded before as far as I am aware, and it shows the strength of an approach that focuses on change as well as difference. It provides us with a clear example of a changing difference—and it indicates greater change in the direction of a more equal domestic division of labor among a group that previously had a more traditionally gendered domestic division of labor.

Tables 5.1 and 5.2 show us a relative picture of changing differences in the division of domestic labor among couples in different socioeconomic groups over a twenty-two-year period. However, the relative domestic division of labor calculation depends on *both* partners' levels of participation; the effect of a decrease in women's time spent in domestic work could be identical to that of an increase in men's time. If the results are analyzed according to *absolute* (rather than relative) amounts of time spent by women and men in couples on the different categories of domestic tasks, a picture familiar from the previous chapter emerges. Overall, the average time women spend in these tasks dramatically declined from 1975 to 1997, while the contribution of men increased, from a much lower base. With respect to difference, this trend is evident for both social class groups. If we focus on the core domestic tasks (cooking and cleaning), we see an overall decrease in women's time from 210 minutes a day to 130 minutes a day, compared with an increase for men from around 20 minutes a day to around 30 minutes a day. But to give some idea of relative scale, this represents a change from women contributing between ten times as much (among professional/technical households) and thirteen times as much (manual/clerical households) as their male partners in 1975 to an average of just over four times as much by 1997. In real terms, men's contribution increased between 10 (professional/technical) to 15 minutes (manual/clerical) a day to an overall average total in 1997 of 30 minutes per day, compared with a decrease of about 80 minutes for women to an overall average total of 130 minutes per day.

The "catching up" in the relative domestic division of labor measure observed for manual/clerical households in table 5.2 is therefore mainly due to differences in the contribution of men. Men in manual/clerical households started from a lower base in 1975 than men in professional/technical households but by 1997 were contributing the same amount on average, while the class ratio remained the same for women across the two survey dates. So for this particular class group at least, it seems that the move toward a less traditionally gendered division of domestic labor has come from an increase in men's contribution, rather than a decrease in women's.

If we introduce employment status (the other main category of difference used here) into the discussion of core domestic work, the men who consistently made the highest contribution (both absolutely and relatively) across both surveys were those in professional/technical households where both partners were employed full time. In 1975 such men spent about 22 percent of the time their female partners spent in cooking and cleaning; by 1997 this had risen to 44 percent (resulting of course from a combination of an increase in men's time spent in such tasks and a decrease in women's). I will return later to this group, who are most likely to fit the criteria of dual-career couples (professional couples in full-time employment). For men in manual/clerical households where both partners were employed full time, the trend was more dramatic (from 13 percent to 31 percent), but due to a lower starting point, the 1997 outcome still reflects a more traditionally gendered domestic division of labor.

In chapter 4, I contrasted domestic tasks in which change in the direction of greater equality of performance was due both to an increase in men's contribution and a decrease in women's (as in the case of the core domestic chores of cooking and cleaning) with other tasks in which we observe increases in the level for both men and women. Among these latter tasks I identified the traditionally feminine-associated child care (although it is sometimes argued that fathers are taking more responsibility in a new age of concern about fatherhood—see chapter 3). If we examine the same relationships (e.g., with employment status and social class), but this time with respect to child care, some interesting features emerge. First, this couple-level British data also supports the conclusion of the macrolevel aggregate data presented in chapter 4 and runs contrary to media panics about neglected children (see also Bianchi 2000). Both women and men showed a marked increase in the time spent in child care between 1975 and 1997. The significance of this increase in child-care activities is discussed more fully in chapter 4—there may be causative factors connected to changes in modes of travel, in leisure activities, and in how people both perceive and report time spent with their children. It is certainly not a feature that has been widely discussed in the current climate of concern about the effect of modern lifestyles (in particular, full-time career employment for women) on the upbringing of children.

As shown also in chapter 4, women contribute substantially more time to child-care tasks than do men, but the magnitude of the sex difference is not as great as for time spent in cooking and cleaning. If we focus more specifically on changing difference, the most notable feature is that the increase in the absolute time spent on child care between the two survey dates of 1975 and 1997 occurs for men in professional/technical households (an increase from 7 to 18 minutes per day, representing a change of around 160 percent). For men in manual/clerical households the increase is also noticeable, although somewhat smaller—from 7 to 14 minutes per day. Therefore while the time spent on child care by men in the two social class groups was equal in 1975, by 1997 a differential had developed, with men from professional/technical households spending slightly more time in child-care activities than their manual/clerical counterparts. For women the equivalent increases were less—though they were in the same direction. There was close to a 70 percent change for women in manual/clerical households (up from 28 to 41 minutes per day), compared with a 90 percent change for women from professional/technical households (up from 32 to 60 minutes per day).

Since these increases in the time devoted to child-care tasks have not been widely reported on, we can only speculate about the reasons. It is possible, for example, that the moral panic around child care has had a more pronounced effect on those from the professional/technical classes— precisely those who are often accused of spending insufficient time with their children due to career considerations—and they have responded by in fact spending more time (or, at least, *reporting* that they are spending more time!) with their children. Bianchi (2000) implies that a recent increase in time spent in child care among men may in some ways be a substitution effect for the increase in women's hours of paid work. If so, we would perhaps expect the effect to be more pronounced among the professional/ technical dual-career group, which is indeed the case. But it is also possible that we are seeing the effect of the relationship between level of education and more caring fathering practices (e.g., Coltrane 1996), reflected here in class differentials in the amount of time spent with children.

I want to return here to the issue I raised at the beginning of the chapter concerning the distribution of couples between subcategories of the relative domestic division of labor measure. This measure of changing difference can give us a direct picture of whether there has indeed been an overall increase between 1975 and 1997 in the percentage of couples with more equal divisions of domestic labor (couples in which the woman contributes less than 60 percent, say, of the overall domestic work time). In table 5.3 we see the distribution of couples according to a set of percentile categories of the relative domestic division of labor measure (i.e., the percentage of domestic work time contributed by the woman). The table is further broken down by couple employment status.

The particular thing to note about table 5.3 is the surprisingly high percentage of couples among the full-time employed households in which the man contributes more time to domestic work (broadly defined to include child care and shopping) than the woman (shown in the first category, labeled 0–49 percent). By 1997, in nearly one-third of couples in which both partners are employed full time, the man is contributing more time to domestic work than the woman. The trend is both substantial and consistent, up from 15 percent of such couples in 1975. Having made the point, it is of course still the case in 1997 that for two-thirds of full-time employed couples, the woman is contributing more to domestic work time than her partner. In addition, we should bear in mind that we are looking here at a sample of couples who define themselves as married or living as married, which also includes some cohabiting couples. The literature tells us that such couples have a more equal division of domestic labor than formally married couples (e.g., Cherlin 1978; Shelton 1992; Gupta 1999), so some of the effect we are seeing may be due to this association with legal marital status.

Table 5.3. Percentage of Couples in Domestic Division of Labor Categories by Employment Status of Partners (percent done by women)*

	Both Full Time			Husband ft, Wife pt			Husband ft, Wife ne		
	1975	1987	1997	1975	1987	1997	1975	1987	1997
0–49	15	20	32	3	6	15	2	6	4
50–59	20	23	26	6	18	9	5	9	17
60–69	17	24	14	13	25	32	10	21	22
70–79	23	22	12	28	33	18	24	26	30
80+	24	17	9	34	41	23	40	59	24
N = 100%	158	104	57	199	120	34	294	118	23

*Among British couples of working age defining themselves as married or living as married
Key: ft = full time; pt = part time; ne = not employed
Source: This table was originally published in Sullivan 2000.

Looking across the employment categories we see, as expected, a higher percentage of couples with more traditionally gendered divisions of domestic labor as the woman's employment status changes from full time, to part time, to not employed. However, if we focus again on changing difference, an inspection of the median, or the modal, category for each group reveals an upward shift over time, indicating a general trend toward a more equally shared model of domestic labor among couples. The modal category for *all* joint employment statuses in 1975 was 80+ (percentage of domestic work time contributed by the woman). During this period, the burgeoning of feminist research on the inequalities of housework began. By 1997 it was 70–79 percent for couples including a full-time employed man and a nonemployed woman, 60–69 percent for couples including a full-time employed man and a part-time employed woman, and 0–49 percent for full-time employed couples. Looking at the extremes of the distribution, an increase over time is evident among all employment status combinations in the first two categories of the distribution when added together (in which the woman contributes only up to 60 percent of the domestic work time). In those employment status combinations where the woman is in paid work (both full time and part time), there is also a clear increase in the percentage of couples in which the man actually contributes more (the first category)—which doubles for couples where both are employed full time (15 to 32 percent) and increases by a factor of 5 (from a lower base) for couples where the woman is employed only part time (3 percent to 15 percent). In addition, a decrease is evident over time in the percentage of couples with a highly traditionally gendered division of domestic work; in all joint employment statuses, there is a decline between 1975 and 1997 in the percentage of couples where the woman contributes 80 percent or more of the domestic work. For full-time employed couples, this decline is monotonic: from just under one-quarter of such couples in 1975 to only 9 percent in 1997.[6]

The overall conclusion is that over the twenty-two-year period covered by the surveys, there has been a general decline in the percentage of couples with more traditionally gendered divisions of domestic labor and an increase in couples with more equal divisions. The increase in the proportion of couples where the man contributes more domestic work time than the woman is particularly striking. There are hints of the possibility of this increase in the literature, but I have not so far heard of any other recording of it based on large-scale data.

Nevertheless, also evident in table 5.3 is the familiar and obvious story that, even among full-time employed couples, the burden of domestic work still falls more heavily on the woman. In particular, for the majority of couples in 1997 in which the woman is not employed full time, the division of domestic work time is still weighted quite heavily on her; when she is employed part time, 41 percent of couples fall into the 70+ categories, and when she is not employed, the equivalent figure is 54 percent of couples.

The last few points raise questions about differences in employment status and egalitarianism in the overall division of labor among couples. For example, in couples where the woman is employed part time or not at all, what is her contribution to the overall work time of the couple, taking paid and unpaid work together? And for full-time employed couples, do the respective hours of paid work of men and women make a difference to who contributes more to domestic work? These considerations suggest a complementary analysis of women's proportion of overall work time (paid and unpaid) in relation to her hours of employment (see table 5.4).

The first point to note from table 5.4 is that the contribution of women to the overall work time (taking paid and unpaid together) of the couple is roughly 50 percent across the time span covered by the three surveys. However, Jacobs and Gerson (1998) note important differences between women in the experience of time pressure. For women who are not

Table 5.4. Proportion of All Work Performed by Women in Couples, by Hours in Paid Work per Week*

	1995	1987	1997
All	0.49	0.49	0.51
0–5	0.47	0.47	0.47
5–30	0.50	0.50	0.52
30–36	0.50	0.52	0.53
36–40	0.52	0.51	0.52
40+	0.53	0.54	0.55

*Among British couples of working age defining themselves as married or living as married
(*Source:* This table was originally published in Sullivan 2000.)

employed, or whose hours of paid work per week are very low, the proportion of overall work time remains a little under parity, at 47 percent. In contrast, as hours of paid work increase, it seems that women, overall, contribute somewhat more than their partners, and the clearest overload occurs for those women who are working full time (forty hours or more per week). At this level of employment, women are working 3 to 5 percent longer than men (taking paid and unpaid work together). Large-scale data suggests the existence of a dual burden here, although the overload is not as high as some researchers (e.g., Hochschild 1989) imply (see also Pleck 1985). One reason for this, as other researchers have proposed, is that women may spend more of their time multitasking (e.g., doing several domestic chores at the same time). Convincing evidence from both quantitative and qualitative empirical research suggests this may be the case; women do indeed spend more of their time in more intensive ways (i.e., doing several different tasks simultaneously) (Sullivan 1997b; Shaw 1998; Bittman and Wajcman 2000; Southerton, Shove, and Warde 2001).

Other suggested explanations for the sense of overload that women experience have referred to the unequal distribution of household tasks in regard to the unpleasantness of chores, with responsibility for the less pleasant tasks, as well as the overall management responsibility, falling to the woman. Cleaning the toilet, for example, continues to be an effective discriminator between women's and men's tasks in the home. In addition, there is some evidence that when women work, on average they work harder than men at any specific task (e.g., Bielby and Bielby 1988). That the overall load in terms of time is more equal than expected among this group of hard-working women may therefore be misleading, since we should also be taking into account the additional feelings of stress associated with multitasking and the performance of unpleasant work.

Summary and Conclusion

While the previous chapter shows overall cross-national changes in men's and women's contribution to aspects of domestic work, this chapter focuses on the question of *changing differences.* I describe changes in the connection between the domestic division of labor and some of the common socioeconomic variables known to be associated with domestic work patterns.

Specifically, this chapter shows the changing connection between the relative domestic division of labor, social class, and employment categories for British couples from 1975 to 1997. In choosing these variables and data, I have certainly neglected many other important and interesting differences between population groups. But what I hope to have demonstrated is the sort of analysis at the quantitative level that we need to begin to describe and understand issues of change within a context of diversity.

First, the overall *changes* support both the findings of the previous chapter and a growing body of other evidence on change. In table 5.1, the increase in the relative importance of men's contribution to domestic work time is reflected in an overall 14 percent drop in the relative domestic division of labor measure among couples (down from 77 percent of domestic work time contributed by the woman to 63 percent). However, the tables tell us about changes while holding constant either family status, or employment status, or class. The question might be asked, can we hold constant the *joint* effects of all these structural changes? In order to achieve this, a multivariate analysis holds constant the changes in family status and couple employment status over the period of the surveys. The overall grand mean for the relative domestic division of labor measure over the survey period from this analysis is 72 percent (i.e., 72 percent of domestic labor time contributed by the woman). This gives us our measure of overall level (consistent with other research). However, if we focus again on change, between the dates of the successive surveys, we still observe a statistically significant decrease of 8 percent in the measure (from 76 percent to 68 percent) while holding constant the effects of the structural variables. From 1975 to 1997, this change represents a decrease of something less than 0.5 percent a year in the relative domestic division of labor measure (although, in fact, all the observed change occurred between 1975 and 1987—between 1987 and 1997 there was no significant difference in level[7]). Again, this estimate may not seem that impressive when considered year on year, but it is the *consistency* of the trend toward men's greater participation in domestic work while holding constant the effect of various structural variables that is worthy of note.

Second, the overall *differences* shown in the tables reflect the known associations between both full-time female employment and higher household social class and a higher relative contribution from the male partner to domestic labor. These connections are already well established in the literature on differences. However, if we consider *changing difference*, we see that over this period the greater *proportional* changes in the contributions of men were observed among manual/clerical class households. It is in these households that the increase in both the absolute and relative contribution of men has been greatest. This "catching up" effect (to a situation in 1997 of parity with their higher-class counterparts) suggests a process similar to those described in accounts of behavioral social changes originating in the upper strata of society and penetrating over time across the socioeconomic spectrum (c.f. Veblen 1967; Bourdieu 1984). If so, it is a rare thing to be able to document such a process quantifiably over a relatively short period of time.

An additional aspect of changing difference presented in this chapter is the changing distribution of couples' division of domestic labor in relation to socioeconomic variables. There was a noticeable growth over this period in the *proportion* of couples in which the woman contributed less than 60 percent of domestic labor time, especially among those couples in which both the man and the woman were employed full time. The conclusion is that there are now more (i.e., a higher proportion of) couples with more equal divisions of domestic labor. In addition, the 1997 finding that in one-third of full-time employed couples the man actually spends *longer* overall than the woman in domestic work tasks may surprise many. Despite the fact that in the corresponding two-thirds of such couples women contribute more of the domestic work time, and ignoring the issue of gender-specific task management, this still represents a substantial change from the 1975 situation. Observing this kind of change at the upper and lower end of the distribution of couples' division of domestic labor underlines the importance of looking in detail at change within subgroups of couples as well as at the overall average picture.

To summarize the aspects of change and changing difference that arise from these analyses, from 1975 through 1997 there has been (1) a clear reduction in gender inequality in the performance of some of the normatively feminine-associated tasks (i.e., an overall *change*); (2) a larger proportional increase in the time contributed by men from lower socioeconomic strata, to a position of parity with those from higher socioeconomic strata; and (3) a substantial increase in couples with a more equal division of domestic labor, especially among the full-time employed (both the latter findings represent *changing differences*).

This chapter concludes the "case for change"—the review of different levels of evidence reported in chapters 3 through 5. As I have emphasized, it is the correspondence in the direction of change between these different levels, the discursive and the quantitative, that provides us with the most convincing indication of meaningful change. To answer a question asked at the start of this chapter, it is evident from the analyses presented here that structural changes in population composition in respect of employment and class status do not account for all the change toward a more equal division of domestic labor, despite the fact that these are identified as two of the main associates of differences in the division of domestic labor. So, if we accept the evidence, the next question is, from where can we trace these changes, and what do they mean in terms of gender relations? In the following section of the book, I discuss some of the main elements of a theorization of changing gender relations in the domestic sphere, which combines elements of the wider discursive context with changes in domestic gender practices, and suggest a possible framework for analysis.

Notes

1. I am indebted to Jonathan Gershuny for the provision of this data set. The 1975 data come from the British Broadcasting Corporation's Peoples' Activity and Daily Life study. This formed part of a long sequence of viewer/listener availability studies carried out periodically by the Audience Research Department of the BBC from the late 1930s on. The national representative sample of 2,710 addresses yielded 3,545 usable diaries and 690 couples for the purposes of this analysis. The 1987 data are from the ESRC Social Change and Economic Life Initiative (SCELI), a large-scale study conducted in England and Scotland in 1986–1987, the second stage of which included a time-use diary study providing diary materials from around 1,300 individuals in households, drawn from an initial random sample of working-age adults. This yielded a sample size of 392 couples. The 1997 data come from a smaller national random sample that constituted the pilot study for the sixth wave of the British Household Panel Survey in 1991, a national longitudinal study of households in Britain. The diaries of 202 couples are included in the present analysis. All the surveys were whole-household, seven-day diary designs (so that design effects would not be expected to make a difference in the results).

2. Only those couples in which both partners met the criterion of 30 minutes per day or less of missing diary data were included.

3. The activities used to define domestic tasks as a whole are cooking and cleaning, child care, shopping, and odd jobs around the house.

4. It should also be noted that sample numbers are lowest in this category.

5. Unfortunately, the 1975 BBC survey collected only a social status indicator based on the interviewer's assessment of the household. Households were coded according to the Market Research Society classification of class, identified by letters from A through E (Market Research Society 1991). Despite the shortcomings of subjective assessment, this designation does at least circumvent the thorny issue of how to classify the social status of households made up of different individuals. In order to minimize the difficulties of interviewer assessment of class, a familiar dual-class classification was adopted for the purposes of these analyses, with social class groups C1, C2, D, and E combined into a manual/clerical category, while groups A and B together make up a professional/technical category.

6. For the other two employment status categories, the situation is slightly more complex; there appears to be an increase in the percentage of highly unequal couples between 1975 and 1987, but a substantial fall by 1997 to only around a quarter of couples (well below the 1975 average).

7. There is an interesting correspondence here with Scott, Alwin, and Brown's 1996 analysis of changing attitudes, where they also report that the pace of change slowed in the 1990s.

PART III
CHANGING GENDER RELATIONS AT HOME

THE INTIMATE CONTEXT: GENDER CONSCIOUSNESS AND INTIMACY

) (

In part III, I return to the spatial location of the book: the home. In the previous chapters I discussed both discursive and quantitative empirical evidence for change. In this and the final chapter I present a theoretical approach that addresses the microlevel processes involved in such changes. I begin by dispelling the cozy image connoted by the word *home*. As a shorthand it serves its purpose, but it is a value-laden word, and the processes I will be referring to are in general not very cozy—they involve complex interactions and negotiations with intimate partners in a context of unequal power, as well as the raising and use of strong emotions. As with much that goes on "at home," they can be difficult and painful . . . and sometimes physically violent.

In this chapter I focus on the domestic sphere, outlining changes in the intimate context at the level of personal relationships and interactions. The previous chapters have revealed consistent trends toward greater equality in the performance of domestic tasks on the large scale. By holding constant the effects of various structural changes over time (family status, employment status, and class), I have shown that changes in these structural variables cannot altogether account for the trend toward greater task equality. We must search for other levels and mechanisms of change, such as changes in values, ideology, and the consciousness of rights. In this final part of the book I identify potential alternative sources of change at a more focused level than that of the wider discursive context (which I discussed in chapter 3), and I relate these potential sources to the microlevel processes and practices that go on within the home.

The different elements that I address here center on the concept of gender consciousness, set within an interaction-based approach derived from the doing gender perspective. This approach, which gives a role to agency by connecting the self-reflexive action of individuals in social interaction with the wider level of (shifting) discourse, is in line with de Lauretis's conception of a "political, theoretical self-analyzing practice" (quoted in Alcoff 1988), in which, in the words of Alcoff, "women can (and do) think about, criticize and alter discourse."

As an empirical example I refer to the possible influence of the so-called therapeutic discourses, both in contributing to changes in gender consciousness and in enabling the development of specific interactional skills. In introducing these ideas, I begin to formulate a framework for understanding changes in gender relations in the domestic sphere, which I develop further in chapter 7. In this formulation, the dialectic between daily interaction and gender consciousness forms the pivot—for within the domestic sphere of a couple relationship, this constitutes the arena for gender relations and practice. When we "do gender" within a relationship, we do it as part of a dialectic process, which involves both a conscious interpretation of the other partner's gender ideology and an interactive process with their respective doing of gender.

Both gender consciousness and the resources—material and emotional/relational—that both partners bring to the interaction feed into the processes of daily interaction. My argument here in brief is that the influence of elements of the wider discursive context such as changing symbolic representations of fatherhood (or motherhood), changing attitudes to gender equality (both discussed in chapter 3), changes in images of intimacy, and the influence of therapeutic discourses (to be discussed in this chapter) simultaneously reflect and can produce changes both in the gender consciousness of either partner (related to an awareness of rights) or in the resources that either partner may bring to the interaction (impacting on aspects of marital power). All this takes place, of course, within an existing structural context of gender inequality. However, since my argument is that change is occurring in elements of this structure, my interest here is to understand actual processes of change at the microlevel. I flesh out this brief synopsis in this and the following chapter.

Doing Gender and Gender Consciousness

I begin with the concepts of doing gender and gender consciousness because they play a central role in the framework of multistranded and recursive causality that I present. The pivot of this framework is the dialectic between daily interaction and gender consciousness. It is within the domain of this dialectic that domestic gender relations and practices are actualized. In previous work (Benjamin and Sullivan 1996, 1999), a colleague and I developed an argument that attempts to combine the doing gender approach with the concept of gender consciousness. The rationale for this combination is that the emphasis within the doing gender approach on daily interaction at the domestic level should be set within a broader theoretical frame, within which processes of change at the wider discursive level are actively conceptualized. Here I build on the framework provided by this combination of gender consciousness and doing gender.

One of the most powerful theoretical arguments about gender relations at home was initially articulated by Berk (1985). In her attempt to explain the lack of domestic conflict found in her research, she proposed the basis for what came to be known as the doing gender argument (West and Zimmerman 1987; West and Fenstermaker 1993). Within this approach, gender is perceived as "situated identities" that are established in each interaction through fulfilling tasks, and interpreted by others as fitting (or not) to the normative definitions of manliness or womanliness. The accomplishment of any housework task is therefore seen and seeable in context as gender appropriate or (purposefully) gender inappropriate. Thus "housework is a mechanism for the production of gender in that household tasks often become occasions for reaffirmation of one's gendered relations to work and to the world" (Berk 1985, 204). The strength of this argument is that it regards domestic arrangements as the product of the recursive relationship between agency and structure (as addressed for example by Giddens 1984, 1991; Bourdieu 1984; Morgan 1985).

Understanding gender as a situational accomplishment provides a basic starting point for discussing the social organization of gender while avoiding essentialist statements implying a normative universal female subject. Moreover, since the existence of gender prior to its production in daily social interactions is not assumed, it has the potential for providing a sensitive framework for addressing processes of change. In her introduction to West and Zimmerman's paper on doing gender, Lorber emphasizes this potential:

> In their view, gender is fundamental, institutionalized and enduring; yet, because members of social groups must constantly (whether they realize it or not) "Do gender" to maintain their proper status, the seeds for change are ever present. (1987, 124)

I argue for combining the doing gender argument with a framework that explicitly addresses those conditions within the wider discursive environment, which could, in combination with the processes of daily interaction, produce meaningful change. By focusing on the various currents of the wider discursive environment, it may be possible to identify various *changing* gender-constructing discourses and to emphasize the significance of the increasing contemporary popularity of discursive alternatives to "hegemonic masculinity" and "emphasized femininity" (Connell 1987). For example, Giddens suggests that the late modern period has seen a burgeoning of "expert systems," or "the pluralization of contexts of action and the diversity of 'authorities'" (1991, 5). Giddens also suggests that an individual's reflexivity and knowledgeability, reflecting in part attributes of power and material resources, reinforce his or her ability to respond to this changing ideological environment.

Cancian has also documented plurality in the ideological environment in the area of couple relationships. In pointing to the emerging blueprint of intimate relationships, which she names interdependence, she maintains that the arena of gendered behavior is currently becoming increasingly more diversified. Growing numbers of the American population, she argues, have developed wider repertoires of behavior that do not fit in with normative gender roles. Under the influence of the interdependence blueprint, it is possible that household tasks, as well as certain forms of intimate communication that used to have a clear gendered character, are no longer as effective as "occasions" for the production of conventional meanings of gender (Cancian 1987). To widen the theoretical focus, recent changes in the concerns of many poststructuralist feminist writers (e.g., Braidotti 1991; Bailey 1993) have expanded analysis beyond the consideration simply of differences *between* women and men in an attempt to encompass the full complexity of difference, not only between women and men but also *among* women and men and *within* individual women and men. The poststructuralist recognition of "a multiple, shifting, self-contradictory identity" and "identity made up of heterogeneous and heteronymous representations of gender, race and class" (de Lauretis, quoted in Braidotti 1991, 281) highlights a fundamental problem with accounts that are unable to deal with discursive plurality.

The theoretical failure of accounts rooted in the description of implicit dichotomized normative gender roles has had, it seems, two implications for the discussion of change. First, such accounts cannot adequately analyze relational processes wherein the possibility of change is contained. The second implication is that such accounts are inherently unable to encompass a *project* for change; no feminist practice can be envisaged from such analyses because no alternative framework is provided as a focus of resistance and potential change. Much poststructuralist feminist theory has emphasized the emancipatory potential of the recognition of plurality. The heterogeneous and heteronymous identities referred to by Braidotti (1991) are perceived and insisted upon as strategy. To ignore plurality therefore not only impoverishes analysis but also negates the possibility of transformation, an issue I will return to in the conclusion. The challenge is to link the focus on daily interaction in the domestic sphere provided by the doing gender approach to a context of discursive plurality, thereby enabling both an analysis of, and a project for, change.

One theoretical frame that does explicitly address the conditions for change is provided by the concept of gender consciousness, described by Gerson and Peiss (1985) as a continuum along which a more generalized gender awareness may be succeeded under certain conditions by a consciousness of the rights (or entitlements) associated with specific gender locations. Gender consciousness thus involves a process of the recognition of rights based on information from the wider society. The rise of feminism, for example, provided new conditions for the development of gender consciousness. Crucially, however, social interaction also has a reciprocal influence on the generation of those rights. According to Gerson and Peiss, the active bargaining or negotiation that women and men engage in on a daily basis is twinned with a notion of domination, in which it is possible to express the ways women are oppressed but may also accommodate or resist this oppression. So aspects of gender practice are linked to gender consciousness via the active generation of rights in social interaction. Finally, a clearly articulated challenge to the existing system of gender relations may emerge, containing an explicit commitment to change. According to Thompson (1993), gender consciousness thus constitutes a central component of our understanding of women's attempts at change. It may be regarded as a critical enabling element in the transformation of the normative boundaries that regulate gender relations.

The concept of gender consciousness as presented by Gerson and Peiss was applied only to women. However, there is no reason why it should not also be applied to men, with some modifications such as a generalization of the argument about rights/entitlements to include responsibilities (e.g., responsible fathering). Thus a generalized gender awareness may develop into a consciousness both of reciprocal rights/entitlements and of reciprocal responsibilities. One likely empirical example of such a link occurs in the literature on divorce and remarriage. For example, Burgess (1998) suggests that certain men recognize better ways of being a father following divorce. On the same topic, the bulk of the literature suggests that remarried couples share the housework more evenly than couples in first marriages, where the domestic division of labor is on average more gendered in nature (Demo and Acock 1993; Ishii-Kuntz and Coltrane 1992; Pyke and Coltrane 1996; Sullivan 1997a). It has been suggested that the main factor here is an increased degree of negotiation between remarried partners, resulting in a greater sharing of housework. The failure of a first marriage may thus lead to change in the normative boundaries regulating domestic gender interaction and practice, for which, according to Thompson, a change in gender consciousness is a critical enabling element. These changes, I suggest, may occur for one or both partners.

It is important to emphasize here that I am not in the main talking about a happy picture of mutual recognition and agreement on change. To return to an earlier theme of the book, change as a process can be slow and difficult. At the level of the couple, an increase in negotiation is perhaps more likely to be an (eventual) outcome of an increase in *conflict*, developing from a growing awareness and consciousness of rights on the part of the woman and subsequently struggled over on a day-to-day basis (see, for example, Kluwer, Heesink, and Van de Vliert 1996). Indeed, one of my central arguments is that this daily struggle by women provides the main motor for changes in household practices. However, this struggle may be occurring in a discursive context of a growing gender awareness among both women and men. I describe research examples of the accomplishment of change within the home in the following chapter.

Intimacy and the Therapeutic Discourses

The concept of gender consciousness as used by Gerson and Peiss may be utilized to describe the potential for change in the domestic sphere in the light of new discourses of intimacy and equality, which also provide new conditions and information for the development of a consciousness of rights and responsibilities. In other words, it is possible to connect arguments about new discourses of intimacy with those about gender consciousness as part of a framework that incorporates both plurality and change. I now turn to the debate around these new discursive elements.

The late 1980s and early 1990s saw the publication of a number of relatively optimistic accounts of changes in personal relationships in the direction of greater intimacy. From within the feminist literature, Cancian (1987) was among the first to provide an account of these changes, while other dimensions were introduced from the literature on late modernity (Giddens 1992; Beck and Beck-Gernsheim 1995; see Smart and Neale 1999 for a recent discussion of writing on the connection between late modernity and intimacy in the context of the family). In this latter literature, a theoretical link was made between changes associated with the late modern period, in particular the growth of individualism, and the development of more intimate and equal relationships. In *The Transformation of Intimacy*, Giddens describes the elements of change as involving a move toward the "pure relationship," one based on self-reflexivity and mutual disclosure between equals. This trend was thought likely to lead to a progressive undermining of gender inequality. In terms of the relationship to late modernity, the changes were linked in particular to the growth of individualism and individualistic values in an age where kinship and community ties are seen as weakening (e.g., Young and Wilmott 1973; Bellah, Madsen, Sullivan, Swidler, and Tipton 1985; Bauman 1987). They are also related to processes of late modernity such as globalization and increasing risk awareness (see Giddens 1991; Beck, Giddens, and Lasch

1994). These arguments can be linked to the concept of gender consciousness through the connection, identified by Skolnick, between the growth of individualism in the late modern period and the "rights revolution": the claiming of rights by disadvantaged groups (1992, 41). Now, according to Gerson and Peiss's original definition of gender consciousness, the recognition of rights is an important component of change. It is through the link between the growth of individualism, and its associated emphasis on self-development, and the recognition and growing awareness of rights that appropriate conditions for change may be created.

The accounts given by Giddens and other authors on late modernity are, of course, not without their critics, in particular writers with a more circumspect approach to the question of changing gender relations. Jamieson (1998), for example, rejects the relatively optimistic account of the relationship between gender, intimacy, and social change given by Giddens, arguing that public stories have changed more in this area than have private lives. In fact it is Cancian who in many ways still provides the account of changing intimacy that is most sensitive to issues of gender and who also comes closest to an approach based on the raising of gender consciousness. Cancian describes the emergence of a new model of interdependency in intimate relationships that contrasts with both the traditional model (in which masculinity is associated with independence and autonomy, femininity with love and caring) and the fully independent model (where both partners pursue autonomy). In this model, self-development, which in the traditional model is the preserve only of the male, and love are mutually reinforcing. The causal connection is made not to individualism per se but to a more androgynous image of love emerging in the 1970s, together with an increased emphasis on self-development for both men and women (Cancian 1987). An addition to this approach, arising from the relative absence of gender power in the account of the issue, was proposed by Smart and Neale (1999), who suggest it is possible to incorporate into the analysis a different concept of power appropriate to the self-development argument. Thus they suggest the introduction of the concept of debilitative power—the attempt to prevent the other from developing or "finding oneself"—as opposed to traditional (physical force) or situational forms of power.

Overall, this and other accounts of changes in intimacy can provide a theoretical background for changes in gender consciousness, but the level of analysis tends to be rather abstract. What is needed in order to ground these accounts in daily interaction and struggle is a focus on the development of the consciousness of rights and of the means to assert them on an ongoing basis—in other words, the development both of gender consciousness and of the tools and skills of daily interaction and negotiation, which can be used as resources in the contestation of power within couples. One example of an enabling environment for both the raising of gender consciousness and the development of appropriate interactional skills is that developed within the human potential movement in psychotherapy, along with the burgeoning self-help literature associated with it:

> The combined emphasis on intimacy and self-development also reflects the influence of popular psychology and the new therapies of the human potential movement, leading some scholars to label new ideals as "therapeutic" images of love. (Cancian 1987, 8)

The therapeutic discourses encompass a range of practices and media at both the professional and popular level: individual therapy and counseling; group or family therapy; self-enhancing workshops; self-help books, tapes, and videos; and media shows and advisory services. The growth in these practices began in the 1960s and has gathered pace since then. Cancian (1987), for example, reports a fifty-fold increase in the membership of the American Association of Marriage and Family Therapy between 1960 and 1985 (from 237 to nearly 12,000 members). There is some compelling evidence that the rise to media prominence of discourses of therapy and self-help brings with it at least intimations of transformation in personal relationships (Cancian and Gordon 1988; Giddens 1992; Crawford 1995; Benjamin 1998). Both in the popular and the social scientific arenas, the increase in writings and in media (more widely defined) in this area bears witness at least to the sketching out of new *ideals* of intimacy, based on reflexivity and disclosure. For example, Cancian documented the content of articles on marriage in high-circulation magazines from 1900 to 1979, measuring the proportion of articles in each decade that endorsed themes of self-fulfillment, flexible roles, intimacy, and open communication. The proportion displaying these themes rises particularly strongly from the 1960s and through into the 1970s. Reviewing the literature from the major sociological and family journals in the

United States from 1960 to 1980 on what she describes as "the trend from role to self" in marriage, Cancian claims to have found virtually no exceptions, noting that the evidence for this trend is especially strong since the late 1960s.

More recently, direct and indirect reference to these aspects of the wider discursive environment can be found in the work of many authors. For example, Illouz claims that what she terms the "therapeutic ethos" should be understood not only in terms of the pervasive influence of individualism but also as providing a dimension of self-observation and self-knowledge (1991, 240). Crawford writes of the self-help industry:

> The quest for self-transformation encouraged by individualistic social science does, at least, give women the message that "Your life is yours to control." And this belief may be necessary and empowering for anyone committed to change. (1995, 179)

A similar message is found in Giddens (1991), where he argues that therapy can be seen as an expression of "generalized reflexivity" that should be evaluated as a "methodology of life-planning." It represents a means by which the individual may acquire a more developed self-understanding and be able to "harmonize present concerns and future projects with a psychological inheritance from the past" (180). Thus, women's access to expert systems or bodies of knowledge can equip them with new self-perceptions and a new awareness about relations with others. Similarly, what Cancian (1987) refers to as the "human potential movement" in the United States plays a significant role in her argument about the development of new blueprints of intimate relationships, based on images of androgynous love.

Of course, many skeptical voices have been raised about the therapeutic discourses, and it is probably fair to say that some of the more optimistic prognoses arising from assessments of their impact have been the result of ideological simplification (see Jamieson 1999). Some of the early arguments include that this perspective had its origins in individualistic utilitarianism and was likely to have a negative effect on personal and family life through the emphasis on individual needs and goals, leading to anomie and breakdown of social bonds (e.g., Bellah 1985; Swidler 1985). Indeed, it was partly on the basis of this reluctance to see the positive side of the self-development framework that Cancian developed her model of interdependence (1987), which emphasizes the potential for mutuality rather than independence arising from this framework. More recently, criticism has been directed at the commercial underpinnings of the self-help literature (Hochschild 1994), and no doubt, as discussed in Morgan (1996), the interests of certain professionals in the promotion of the therapeutic discourses have also played a role in its rise to media prominence. However, while being perhaps ambivalent in some of its cultural messages (Simonds 1992), these discourses at least take the possibility of change in gender consciousness as a major premise.

In addition, though, an important aspect of the therapeutic discourses as an example of the connection to gender practices within the home is that they can facilitate the development of interpersonal skills and be used as active resources within relationships. Indeed, one of the major messages is that people can develop and improve their interactional skills. Examples of such skills might include change-directed negotiating skills, the ability to express thoughts and feelings more clearly, and the controlled use of anger in conflictual situations. I referred already to the simultaneous importance of changes in gender consciousness and of the development of interactional skills for accomplishing concomitant change in practices. Despite criticism in some of the literature directed at the actual impact of such skills, such messages from the therapeutic discourses are significant, at least in enabling feminist ideas regarding direct conflict and women's empowerment to be brought into the intimate situation (Cancian and Gordon 1988).

In the papers written with Orly Benjamin that I referred to at the start of the chapter, we used the example of therapeutic discourses. We argued that direct and indirect exposure to these discourses can play an enabling role in the accomplishment of change via *both* an increased gender consciousness and the development of specific interactional and emotional skills, which we termed relational resources (as an equivalent to the more familiar and widely analyzed material resources). The development and deployment of these skills in daily interaction is reciprocally connected to a changing gender consciousness, playing a role in both the desire and the ability to accomplish change. However, most research has been devoted to the influence of material or structural resources, such as women's relative or absolute income. This literature has made a major contribution to our understanding of the relationship between marital power and women's differing material resources (e.g., Sanchez 1993; West and Fenstermaker 1993; Pyke 1994). However, it is only relatively recently that the significance of the emotional dimension, broadly defined, has become part of the main research agenda in this area (e.g., Hochschild 1979, 1989; Thompson 1993), and most research within this area has focused on the use of emotional resources such as anger or love (e.g., Duncombe and Marsden 1993; Benjamin 1998). Relatively little direct attention has been given to the issue of differing relational resources. However, we argue that material or structural resources are likely to be mediated by a combination of gender consciousness and relational resources in their effects on interactional processes.

In addition to the structural resources that are known to have an effect on marital power and the division of domestic labor within the home (e.g., as described in the previous chapter, women's employment status, their educational level, and their absolute and relative incomes), we need to take account of other resource dimensions. For instance, women who are exposed (through professional development activities, personal counseling, reading, and so on) to influences at the institutional level that promote the development of reflexivity and self-awareness in intimate relationships are more likely to acquire the relational resources necessary to achieve change in gender practices in the home (Benjamin and Sullivan 1996, 1999). I present some of the findings of this and related research in more detail and develop some of these arguments further in the following chapter.

Summary and Conclusion

To summarize, I am proposing an approach that is constructed on the linkages between several different layers of analysis. The pivot is the dialectic between daily interaction (affected by the development and deployment of relational resources) and changing gender consciousness, which is affected by and simultaneously affects wider discursive influences. Incorporated into the theoretical frame is a recognition of the simultaneously *constituted* and *constitutive* nature of day-to-day interaction, into which potential elements of change are being introduced at different levels of the analysis. I will subsequently refer to this interaction as "embedded" in order to emphasize its located nature within a wider discursive context. In the following chapter, I develop this theoretical framework for understanding change in the domestic sphere by expanding on the concept of embedded interaction and its significance for change, including the presentation of various research examples that have specifically focused on the constructive possibilities of daily interaction in the production of change.

CHANGE AT HOME: RESEARCH EXAMPLES AND A FRAMEWORK

) (

Thus far, in my discussion of the various elements involved in this multilayered account of change, what has been absent is a direct focus on the microlevel. In this chapter I address processes of change in gender relations in the domestic sphere, with the focus on what I have called "embedded interaction." I begin with a discussion of the importance of individual (inter)action in both the reproduction and the production of structures, noting how such an approach fits into the recent integrative perspectives on gender (Risman 2004). I then ask how we can identify processes of change in gender relations occurring among couples in their daily interaction; in other words, what particular dimensions and concepts of interaction might be useful in the identification of change? Next I describe some research examples that focus explicitly on the accomplishment of change, before providing in the final section a model and more fully developed description of embedded interaction.

By embedded interaction, I refer to daily interaction that has a dialectic relationship with gender consciousness, is affected by the material and relational resources of each partner, and is (recursively) embedded within a wider discursive context. The epistemological starting point of this approach is that in an analysis of what facilitates change it is not enough to refer only to wider social and political factors; we need also to take account of the day-to-day processes of interaction on which these factors play.

Connell emphasizes this point in relation to the construction of masculinities:

> Masculinities are neither programmed in our genes, nor fixed by social structure, prior to social interaction. They come into existence as people act. They are actively produced, using the resources and strategies available in a given social setting. (2000, 12)

In the approach presented here, change in gender relations at home arises through processes of interaction in a context both of changing gender consciousness and of change in relational resources, primarily those of women. However, as I have previously argued, a focus on microlevel processes of change has to an extent been absent from the literature, since researchers have tended mainly to apply themselves to theorizing women's consent and adaptation to their position as the caregivers in their families rather than their attempts to alter their domestic arrangements (see De-Vault 1991; Komter 1989; Thompson 1993; Duncombe and Marsden 1993). Even in studies of "sharing" couples (e.g., Coltrane 1989; Doucet 1992; Schwartz 1994; Risman 1998), the *process* by which sharing might be achieved remains largely uninvestigated because the participating couples usually present themselves as intending to share from the starting point of their relationships. Relatively few studies focus on couples that have undergone or are undergoing processes of change or describe the detail of the interactional processes involved.

But by focusing on the level of interaction, I do not intend to be dismissive of the impact of direct or organized political forces on the stimulation of change (e.g., the role of the feminist movement or the efforts that have been made by organizations and groups in the public arena to advance the cause of women). The point about embedded interaction is that interaction occurs within a wider discursive context, with which it has a recursive relationship. Therefore, political action of this kind (collective agency) in the public arena can play an important part not only in struggling for and winning political and economic gains for women but also in feeding into wider discourse, and thus into the gender consciousness of both men and women. For example, changes in linguistic meaning, which I discuss in chapter 3, have often been directly politically inspired—hence the dismissive label of "political correctness"—but they do have a wider effect by feeding through into both gender consciousness and (nonlinguistic) behavior. The point is that there is wide recognition in the literature of the importance of women's collective agency in the public sphere (Walby 1997), but not so much recognition of the political importance of daily interaction in the private sphere in the accomplishment of change.

So the argument here is that in order to investigate the possibilities of change, we should be examining the specific interplay of gender consciousness, relational resources, and material circumstances in their concrete, interactional manifestations. The definitions and descriptions of these concepts are more fully developed in chapter 6, but essentially the attempt to address this interface between different levels of analysis is grounded in the idea that an understanding of possibilities of change in the sphere of gender relations necessarily involves both interactional and institutional dimensions. The recognition of the interpenetration of these dimensions, and their reciprocal influence in the production of change, is not new in gender studies—"the gender perspective simultaneously emphasizes the symbolic and the structural . . . the interactional and the institutional levels of analysis" (Marx Ferree 1990, 868)—but the attempt to derive integrative models describing the components and articulations of the different dimensions, such as those of Risman (1998, 2004) and Connell (2002), is more so. What has not been attempted to any extent is to provide concrete empirical examples of the articulation between different layers of these analytic models in the description of actual processes of change.

One of the things I contribute in this chapter is a discussion and documentation of some examples of research that have described processes of change from the perspective of daily interaction in the home, together with an attempt to relate these changes to wider discursive environments. In the literature on equity in household relations and practices, interaction has long been recognized as significant (see, for example, Thompson 1991 on the emergence of women's sense of fairness from interaction), but far fewer studies have directly empirically addressed the interactive processes involved. Before moving to the research examples, I want to spend a bit of time on the issue of what elements of interactive processes are relevant to change. The question is, what would we actually be looking for in daily interactive processes between women and men at home that would indicate the possibility of change? Here again the work of Gerson and Peiss is useful in the identification of the significance of both negotiation and boundaries as markers of change. In this approach, negotiation relates to how women and men, from an initial base of relative resources, bargain for privileges and position. To account for issues of structural and marital power, Gerson and Peiss (1985) twin this notion of negotiation with domination, which refers to the ways women are oppressed and may accommodate or resist such oppression. Risman has also drawn attention to the importance of negotiation in changing patterns of interaction in her own version of a multilevel account of change (see chapter 1): "Rejecting contemporary expectations and negotiating new ways of interacting begins the process of forging new structures" (1998, 153).

The importance of boundaries to the analysis of gender relations is that they demarcate normative divisions of behaviors and attitudes, permitting the identification of points of dynamic change when they are shifted. There may be large boundaries, as between work and leisure, public and private. But there are also smaller boundaries regulating, for example, the domestic division of labor or "talk and no-talk" zones in the marital conversation (Coltrane 1989; Benjamin 1995; Zvonkovic et al. 1996). The elements of interaction—negotiation and the maintenance or shifting of boundaries—are linked to gender consciousness in a recursive way: Changes in gender relations occur along the three dimensions of boundaries, negotiation/domination, and consciousness; change in any one variable elicits change in the other two (Gerson and Peiss 1985).

Thus negotiation may permit adjustment of boundaries "either preceded, accompanied or followed by an alteration in consciousness" (323). For example, a growing awareness of the right to equality may lead to a change in techniques of negotiation, such as the introduction of controlled anger, which might effect a change in domestic work practices.

Possibilities of Change: Some Research Examples

In the examples taken from my work with Orly Benjamin, the interplay of gender consciousness, relational resources, and material circumstances in their interactional manifestations was the research goal, and the concepts of negotiation and boundaries were used directly as markers of changing gender relations in the home (Benjamin and Sullivan 1996; 1999). In other examples, the drawing out of these relationships was less direct, but their significance is that they all involve detailed description at the level of daily interaction of the accomplishment of (or the failure to accomplish) change. Instead of accepting as given the current division of domestic labor among couples, all these examples place an emphasis on process. The starting assumption is that it is not enough simply to posit and investigate a continuum of domestic arrangements, ranging from the very unequal to the equal, because the position of individual couples over time can shift significantly. Of course, one of the assumptions here is that we are looking at couples whose relationships survived processes of change; those who struggled with but who failed to change might have ultimately failed to survive as couples. Even though evidence suggests that remarriages are characterized by greater sharing, this is not really the point. I have already put forth the case that change *is* occurring on a number of different levels—what this chapter and the research examples I present are about is understanding these processes of change where and when they occur within the home. Among the issues addressed are the boundary points over which couples experience conflict, women's conscious strategies for the stimulation of change, and the resources and power from the wider environment that each partner may bring to bear in negotiation and conflict in relation to their respective (and potentially changing) gender ideologies. So in addition to describing the (unequal) practices of the division of household labor, these studies also point to how it is possible to theorize processes of change as they occur in daily interaction. This possibility in turn enables an analysis that can relate these processes to changes in wider structures of gender ideology and gender consciousness.

Most of the studies referred to in the following discussion rely on depth interviewing techniques to explore processes of change at the level of daily interaction. Interviews were conducted either with women in couples, as in Benjamin and Sullivan (1996, 1999) and Pesquera (1997), or with both partners, as in Schwartz (2001). Despite the information they provide on process, they are subject to criticism based on the known problems of interview methodology, including recall difficulties and the ex post facto rationalization of events and feelings. Outstanding among the work of authors who have been concerned with the actual observation and description of day-to-day interactions in the household is that of Hochschild (1989, 1997). Her method of family ethnography, although potentially perhaps the most effective in that it permits observation of processes of interaction both in situ and in real time, is nevertheless extremely time consuming. In relation to the length of time over which interviewed couples often describe any significant change as occurring (which may be over years), it is clearly problematic as a methodology. Undertaken over relatively short periods of time, as is only practicable, it will therefore have the tendency to reinforce ideas of stability rather than change.

Doucet's "household portrait" technique introduces a somewhat different methodological tool that is explicitly designed to allow couples to discuss how their domestic division of labor has changed over the years. The technique was devised in explicit recognition that not only difference but also change is an element of the household division of labor. While several authors had argued that there was "outstanding" stability in the gender pattern of household labor, Doucet contended that the experience of this stability needed to be understood from the perspective of respondents themselves. She therefore developed a participatory technique for facilitating couples' discussion of their experiences, allowing her to metaphorically follow these experiences "through the years of their lives and into the rooms of each household" (1996, 161). The technique was based on visual cues (the couples constructed a "household portrait" based on colored pieces of paper representing different household tasks and responsibilities). These visual cues provided a reference point for the discussion of household life: "It [the household portrait] encouraged discussion, analysis, debate, agreement and disagreement over how each household's particular division of labor had changed over the years" (169).

So although problems of recall may be evident, the use of visual cues and the debate aspect of the technique appear to stimulate couples to remember and tell the detailed story of the processes of conflict and change that they have experienced. For example, among her interviewees Laura and Mark discuss how they have kept trying, with some admitted difficulties, to share household tasks more equally over their twenty-five years of marriage. Another woman (Anna) talks about gradual shifts over the past ten years, with some "more dramatic" shifts beginning five years ago in the "area of shared enterprise" (165). While interviewing couples together may tend to underrepresent the extent of conflict, it efficiently reveals both the amount of change and the detailed processes involved. One of Doucet's central points is that the picture we are accustomed to receiving of outstanding stability in gender divisions of household labor is only a partial one that fails to take into account the complex explanations used by women and men to describe the "daily, weekly, monthly, and yearly layers of difference which may move and change" (166).

In Benjamin and Sullivan 1996, we wrote about differences in the interaction between couples and the conditions under which the "opening up of the marital conversation" can underpin the development of more flexible domestic divisions of labor. The study on which the analyses were based was conducted by Orly Benjamin in England in 1991–1992, and further details of both the methodology and the development of the argument may be found in Benjamin 1995. The data included both questionnaire responses and depth interviews with four groups of Caucasian professional women: head teachers, social workers, marriage guidance counselors, and chartered accountants.[1] It is among such groups of middle-class employed professional women, who enjoy relatively high levels of earnings both absolutely and in relation to their husbands' earnings, that there is the most evidence in the literature for a more equal domestic division of labor (e.g., Edgell 1980; Dancer and Gilbert 1993; Baxter 1993; Heath and Bourne 1995; Coltrane 1996).

In this study, those women who had struggled and succeeded in achieving some change in the domestic division of labor emphasized the importance of negotiation in supporting the process of change. Using the criterion of "increased flexibility" in the domestic division of labor as the major indicator of change reflected this focus. At the level of women's experience, a woman who has to manage the strains of the "second shift" on her own in the context of lack of cooperation shares little in common with a woman who can negotiate freely with and make direct requests of her partner and enjoy his cooperation in a range of situations (Benjamin 1995). Therefore the question asked was, under what conditions can the flexibility of domestic arrangements increase so that more tasks can be negotiated and allocated according to need? For some egalitarian couples, a different picture might have emerged had there been an attempt to study them at earlier stages in their relationship. And indeed, it appears that among these different groups of professional women in Britain, a not-commonly recognized diversity prevailed, with some women suggesting they had no hope of introducing any change into their relationships or their domestic divisions of labor, and other women describing processes of change actually taking place. Examples include a woman who chose to pursue direct conflict to the point where she made her husband realize that the relationship would not continue unless he changed. And indeed he accepted several domestic tasks as his duty. Another respondent achieved an agreement with her husband whereby she accepted the burden of commuting while he accepted the responsibility of afternoon child care and evening meals (Benjamin 1995).

The importance of negotiation also emerges strongly in other research. For example, Schwartz's study is slightly different in that it takes "peer marriages" as its starting point (i.e., couples with an approximately equal domestic division of labor). Nevertheless, strong emphasis is put on the importance of communication and discussion to resolve differences. Schwartz writes that in matters of disagreement, most couples "ultimately . . . followed their usual pattern of talking until agreement was reached. What usually forced them to continue to communicate and reach a joint answer was their pledge to give the other partner equal standing in the relationship" (2001, 191).

It can be argued that a focus on interaction among couples with an existing commitment to equality does not directly address the issue of change and may present too painless an account of the negotiation process. Most of Schwartz's couples, for example, "placed particular emphasis on equity and sharing" (188). But the processes of negotiation leading to change can of course also be painful; the overcoming of boundaries governing talk and no-talk areas and the introduction of emotion into discussion are potentially fraught with difficulty and distress (as in the above example of direct conflict). Goodnew and Bowes (1994) note that, even among couples characterized by acceptance of the possibility of negotiation and who had negotiated a different division of labor, the process of negotiation was often painful—it was difficult for women to talk about household work without bringing issues of power to the surface. The initial result of women's attempts to introduce these topics was therefore often conflict (see also Kluwer, Heesink, and Van de Vliert 1996).

These examples highlight the significance of women's contributions to the accomplishment of change, since it is assumed to be women who introduce these topics in the talk zone, facing conflict in doing so. The importance of women's agency and their gender consciousness in the introduction of change is also evident in other examples. The women who reported achieving change pointed out the importance of their own belief in the possibility of changing aspects of the relationship and establishing some mutual commitment to its improvement (Benjamin 1995). Under these conditions, partners who were unwilling to cooperate in the introduction of change in the earlier phase of the relationship actually took to the task and fulfilled it seriously. From research into the relationship between the ideology and practice of the division of domestic labor among Chicana workers, Pesquera describes how some of her women respondents used a combination of gender strategies, including both an "underground approach" (retraining, coaching, praising) and more directly confrontational techniques, in order to accomplish change. Pesquera concludes that "a strong relationship emerged between women's willingness to engage in 'political struggle' and the level of male involvement in household labor" (1997, 218).

The relationship between women's engagement in struggle and male involvement referred to in the previous quotation is described as existing in addition to factors such as the lack of a substantial earnings gap and the practical demands of the women's careers—in other words, above and beyond more conventional research considerations both of marital power (e.g., as indicated by relative earnings) and of the practical contingencies of women's employment. It is also clear in Schwartz's study, at least for some of these couples, that the woman had been the main agent in the desire for and the achievement of equality: 40 percent of women cited feminism and the desire for a nonhierarchical relationship as a factor, while this was true of only of 20 percent of men. "Quite a few" men said they had no strong feelings about an egalitarian marriage and simply "followed their wife's lead" (188).

In 1999 we followed up our previous paper with an analysis of the relationship between gender consciousness, relational resources, and gender relations in the home (Benjamin and Sullivan 1999). The empirical model was operationalized in terms of measures of exposure to therapeutic discourse, interpersonal skills, openness in marital communication, and the domestic division of labor among the same groups of professional women.[2] We argued that direct and indirect exposure to therapeutic discourses can play an enabling role both in the desire and the ability to accomplish change via both an increased gender consciousness (leading to an awareness of rights) and the development of specific interactional skills. We further argued that relational resources (such as interactional skills), like material resources, can act as important facilitators of change in aspects of intimate relationships (specifically, in aspects of marital communication and the domestic division of labor).

And indeed, relational resources acquired through professional life were directly perceived by some women as contributing to the successful negotiation of change in their marital relationships. For instance, of the thirteen marriage guidance counselors interviewed, three confidently attributed a significant change in their marital relationships to their counseling training, while another six described changes they had experienced as being related primarily to individual therapy (often undertaken during or as a consequence of their professional training).[3] These women described examples of success in changing the boundaries of marital communication, such that issues that could not be discussed earlier in the relationship (e.g., housework) were brought by the interviewees into the marital conversation in a way that enabled their discussion, and often this seemed to enable change in the related aspect of the relationship (see Benjamin 1995). The survey data support this conclusion: Of 230 respondents who reported that it had become easier to go against their partners' expectations, more than half ($N = 130$) related the change to the impact of their occupational life. Of those who made this connection, 60 percent were either marriage guidance counselors or social workers, whose occupational training involves the development of specific relational resources.

We also performed a multivariate statistical analysis on this data, comparing the effect of women's material resources (as measured by years in full-time employment) to that of their relational resources[4] on the extent of their partners' participation in domestic work. We showed that the effect of relational resources on partner participation is still significant even when holding constant the effect of years of full-time employment (Benjamin and Sullivan 1999, table 5). In terms of the relative contribution of the two effects, the relational resources of women accounted for about one-third of the explained variation in partner participation, compared with two-thirds for the measure of material resources. But in addition to this overall comparison of the contribution of different resources, the effect of a high level of relational resources was largest among the group with the greatest number of years in full-time employment. In other words, the impact of relational resources is higher when the level of material resources is also high. Thus it appears from this analysis not only that relational resources are important as facilitators of change over and above the known impact of material resources but also that there is a reinforcement effect between the two, such that women with higher levels of material resources benefit more from the acquisition of relational resources. This interaction effect between material and relational resources derives theoretical support from Gerson and Peiss's assessment that (gender) "consciousness . . . is the outcome of processes of negotiation and domination *as well as the result of women's structural location*. . . . [It] influences processes of negotiation and domination, and ultimately, the boundaries shaping gender relations" (1985, 325) (my italics).

Other researchers have looked at the issue of change with a focus on differences in professional lives in a similar vein. The emphasis on occupation here is not coincidental, since occupation represents a difference between women that acts as a mediating connection between the worlds of the public and the private, strongly influencing both the relational and the material resources that women command within the household. In illustration of this point Crompton, in a cross-national analysis of attitudes and equality in the home among women doctors and bankers, found a more equal domestic division of labor among bankers than among doctors, despite the similarity in material circumstances. She attributes this finding to the managerial training of bankers, by implication including negotiation and personnel skills, as opposed to the professional training of doctors (Crompton and Harris 1999).

The results of other studies are also interesting in this respect. In Schwartz's research, she admits that she expected most of her peer marriages to be "yuppie" or "post-yuppie" professional couples. What she found is that most of them were in fact from more modest middle-class occupations such as small-business owners, social workers, teachers, and health professionals. Missing from her sample were high-earning, high-status professionals such as litigators, investment bankers, and high-status doctors (2001). Her surmise is that a career fast-track with high material rewards in these professions is inimical to the development of egalitarian relationships. This conclusion is supported by Blair-Loy's research on women in the male-dominated worlds of stockbroking and finance, where successful professional women may subcontract their traditional domestic responsibilities but continue to be "haunted by" the cognitive, normative, and emotional power of a "family devotion" schema (Blair-Loy and Jacobs 2003) and where gender inequalities in the home are reinforced by the increasing time demands of the job in a globalizing market (Blair-Loy 2001). Interestingly, among the four groups of professional women that we studied, chartered accountants have both the lowest levels of exposure to therapeutic discourse and the most traditional domestic divisions of labor (Benjamin 1995; Benjamin and Sullivan 1999).

The use of occupation as a key independent variable in the study of the domestic division of labor is a relatively new development, but its importance and significance seem to lie in the interplay, illustrated in the previous examples, between the level of material and relational resources accruing from women's differing occupational lives. Among both Caucasian English women (Benjamin and Sullivan 1999) and Chicano American women (Pesquera 1997), a relationship by occupation is found in relation to how successfully women were able to alter the distribution of household labor, reflecting differentials in material and relational resources. Significantly, in Pesquera's study the importance of struggle in achieving change was also found to be mediated by the differing gender ideologies of the different class groups: Professional and blue-collar workers started out with higher expectations of equality than did the clerical group and had attitudes that were less strongly linked to male and female roles in the house. This point emphasizes the significance of perceptions of equity and fairness in a relationship, as discussed by Thompson (1991), Pyke and Coltrane (1996), and Sanchez and Kane (1996). Where women do not perceive their situation as unequal, or where they have fewer expectations of equality, the stimulus for direct conflict is considerably reduced (Lennon and Rosenfield 1994; Thompson 1991). It is in relation to this point that the concept of gender consciousness plays a part, since it is strongly linked to differences in expectations and perceptions of rights.

Embedded Interaction: The Framework

In introducing the concept of embedded interaction in the previous chapter, I referred to the interaction and negotiation that takes place between partners in specific contexts of gender consciousness, relational and material resources, and the wider discursive environment. According to this perspective, it is thus possible to see gender relations as being simultaneously and interpenetratingly constructed at the institutional level *and* negotiated within individual relationships in such a way as to permit the possibility of change. In previous chapters I introduced and discussed the elements of embedded interaction more fully. In this chapter I tried to trace empirical examples of their possible influences in changing gender practices around the domestic division of labor.

In this brief review, I have not been able to describe in detail all the connections between the different elements of this approach. It may be helpful therefore to present the multilayered recursive framework of embedded interaction as a diagram in which the analytic elements I refer to are set in relationship to each other. In figure 7.1 the double-ended arrows represent interpenetrating, recursive relationships. Here the wider discursive context can be seen as both affecting and being affected by gender consciousness, which in turn is recursively related to relational resources (themselves also affected by the wider discursive context, as in the example of therapeutic discourses). What I have termed embedded interaction constitutes the heart of this complex of relationships. It refers to the dynamic processes of the daily interaction between partners, embedded

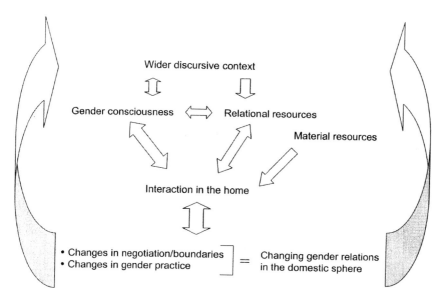

Figure 7.1. A Multilayered Recursive Framework for Analyzing Change ("Embedded Interaction")

within their social and discursive context. As I have argued, the daily processes of interaction have a recursive relationship, both with gender consciousness and with relational resources, and are also affected by the material resources of each partner. Given the right circumstances, change can occur over time in the pattern of daily interaction that constitutes domestic gender relations and practice. If enough of this kind of change occurs at this level, it can in turn produce changes in the wider discursive context, through the recursive relationship with changing gender consciousness. This process is indicated by the large arrows at the sides, which indicate the effect of changing gender practices and relations in the domestic sphere on the wider discursive environment.

Notes

1. For purposes of comparison, only Caucasian women were included in the survey. The question of whether the same relationships exist for professional women from nonhegemonic ethnic backgrounds is a fascinating one, yet to be addressed.

2. It was hypothesized that women with the most systematic exposure to such discourse would be professional women who came into contact with these issues through their employment (marriage guidance counselors and social workers). In order to fairly compare access to therapeutic discourses between women, it was therefore necessary to use other professional women as a comparison group (see Benjamin 1995).

3. The direct effect of therapy on negotiation (although not, in this instance, associated with a successful change in gender relations within an ongoing relationship) is also directly referred to by Smart and Neale when they give the example of a woman expressing the importance of "therapy and all sorts of reading" in her abilities to articulate in negotiation with her ex-husband (1999, 142).

4. Relational resources were based on the self-reports of the respondents and calculated as a scale. The scale was then dichotomized for the purposes of the analysis into high and low categories (above and below the mean value).

CONCLUSION: A PROJECT FOR CHANGE?

) (

I have presented an argument, and a theoretical framework, for analyzing change in gender relations in the home. That (slow) change is happening is consistent both with the large-scale empirical documentation of changes in practices around the domestic division of labor and with evidence from changes in attitudes and symbolic representations of masculinity. It is the combination of evidence from these different levels (the discursive and the quantitative) that provides so convincing an argument. Yet until relatively recently, unlike changes in the public sphere, changes in the domestic sphere received rather little attention in the literature. This is certainly in part due to the fact that the processes of change I describe are slow; they are not easy to identify or analyze; they do not look like changes of the "upheaval" kind that we commonly associate with late modernity; and they look even less like a "transformation" of the kind that has occurred in the public arena. Nevertheless, I argue that change can be slow and still be significant. In this respect I believe more strongly in the optimistic view of incremental change than do some other authors who have written in a similar vein.

One goal of feminist research has been the empowerment of subjects, and I have in the past been criticized for presenting too optimistic an outlook, which might lead to complacency. I would respond that I am not at all arguing for complacency: Change is *not* inevitable but rather is always conditional on the interaction between structure and action. Doing gender and the processes of interaction that it includes reproduces and concretizes hegemonic gender structures (Risman 1998). However, under

111

the right conditions, in a context of plurality, shifting gender discourses and consciousness, these processes contain within themselves the possibility for effecting change. This possibility is increasingly recognized in the literature—it forms an important theme both of Risman's analysis of the interpenetrating relationship of gender structure with the actors who both shape and are shaped by it (Risman 1998) and of Connell's concept of "configurations of gender practice," in which gender practices as dynamic processes can have a transformative effect on gender relations (Connell 2000).

Thus individual actors are also active agents of change, but because of existing hegemonic structures (which are themselves also fluid), the process may not be a rapid or an easy one. I therefore regard this approach as a call for action at the personal level. By focusing on daily interaction not just as a reproductive but also as a potentially transformative process, it is possible to conceive of women's everyday struggles as a constitutive part of a wider social process, implicated with slow changes both in gender consciousness and practice. In the absence of determined policy changes focused on the domestic sphere, we can expect such changes to continue to be slow. But an important political question must be how we can reintegrate change as a political project, not just in the public domain but also at the individual level. The message from the focus on the level of daily interaction here is that everyday struggles around gender can also make a difference, and the changes they produce can be theorized in a meaningful way. In the poststructuralist critique of subjectivity, this is, I believe, a message that feminism has partially lost. We should give theoretical recognition to the potential change that can occur within the context of everyday processes of interaction between women and men, girls and boys, in (and out of) households. We should acknowledge that, while part of that everyday process involves a struggle to justify or disguise existing inequalities (a well-documented creation of a kind of "false consciousness"—Jamieson 1999), another part of it also involves a struggle for change. In the literature to date, the former has been reported much more widely and has received much more theoretical attention than the latter, and it was in part to fill this lacuna that this book was conceived.

In some ways this argument can be seen as a return to the call of early second-wave feminism that "the personal is political." We should resist the fatalistic assertion that men and women come from different planets and are thus doomed to permanent miscommunication, along with the other worn aphorisms that "you can't teach an old dog new tricks," or "you can lead a horse to water but you can't make it drink." Wrong. One of the lessons of postmodern feminism is that we all perform a multitude of different roles, and we all have multiple selves. As well as the tendency to become stuck in particular roles in certain situations, we all carry within ourselves the capacity for adaptation and change. As feminists, therefore, we should, instead, be sending the message that every little bit helps. Every small struggle to redefine boundaries, to open up the marital conversation, to negotiate change in domestic gender practices contributes in the end to wider processes of transformation. As the research of Pesquera (1997) and Benjamin (1998) informs us, both the willingness and the skills to engage in struggle at this level are important determinants of the accomplishment of change. To formulate the operationalization of this call is much more difficult, but I like Pesquera's description of her respondents' combination of gender strategies in the accomplishment of change in the home, including both the "underground approach" (consisting of retraining, coaching, praising) and more directly confrontational techniques, such as overt nagging, slowdowns, and even strike action. So we can, of course, learn useful things from each other's writing. We can even learn bits and pieces from the therapeutic discourses without having to buy the whole message: how to communicate more openly or effectively, how to encourage/cajole a partner to share more equally in the household chores, how to use and control our anger more constructively when this doesn't happen. It was never going to be an easy process, and it is going to be continue to be a slow one, but the argument of this book is that things are moving—and mostly in the right direction.

Finally, I believe the key to a theoretical analysis that is able to incorporate the idea of this kind of change lies in the integration of different levels of analysis, as manifest in concrete empirical examples. On the one hand, it is critical to identify changes at the level of the ideologies and discourses that structure gendered interactions. Analyses of middle-level variables such as attitudes has indicated substantial shifts across, and even within, generations in attitudes toward issues of equality within the home. But how these attitudes are shaped, and how they translate into (inter)action, is far less well researched. On the other hand I have suggested that, despite some justifiable criticism, the burgeoning of media on therapeutic discourses may be regarded as indicative of a change in representations and conceptions of intimacy. The huge growth of literature on masculinity and fatherhood over the 1990s is also suggestive of change. Empirical observations of changes in practice within the home, as measured by the time spent on different domestic tasks, are also by now well documented. But again, far less is known about the processes that led to these changes at the microlevel. At this level, the key lies in the detailed analysis of processes of change as they occur in day-to-day intimate interaction. Important here are observations not just of changes in practice but also of the resources, processes, negotiations, and struggles that have led to changes, as described by the actors themselves. Combining these levels is the most difficult theoretical task of all. What I have attempted in this book is to offer some suggestions for a framework for thinking about this combination, in which insights derived from the doing gender approach, including a full recognition of the transformative potential of daily interaction, may be combined with a conception of gender consciousness (Gerson and Peiss 1985). Change in gender consciousness, in a process I refer to as embedded interaction, can itself be linked in a recursive system both to the wider discursive context (moving up the level of analysis) and moving down to changes in day-to-day interaction in the home.

APPENDIX: COEFFICIENTS FROM OLS REGRESSION ANALYSIS

) (

Table I. Minutes Per Day in Four Broad Time-Use Categories: OLS Regression Coefficients for Women and Men

WOMEN	Paid	Unpaid	Leisure	Personal	Total
Aged <40, no kids	45 **	−64 **	3	16 **	0
Kids 0–5	−21 **	104 **	−73 **	−10 *	0
Kids 6–15	2	42 **	−35 **	−8 *	0
Older no kids (ref)					
Full-time empl.	289 **	−140 **	−127	−22 **	0
Part-time empl.	151 **	−72 **	−73 **	−6	0
Non/unemployed (ref)					
Canada	24 **	−5	−20 *	0	0
Denmark	17 *	−58 **	76 **	−34 **	0
Netherlands	−20 *	5	11	4	0
UK	9	−3	−24 **	19 **	0
USA	21 *	29 **	−62 **	11 *	0
Finland (ref)					
1961–1971 (ref)					
1972–1981	13 *	−37 **	14 *	10 *	0
1982–1995	11	−34 **	15 *	7 *	0
(Constant)	15	361 **	508 **	556 **	1440
Adj R Square	.41	.35	.17	.05	

MEN	Paid	Unpaid	Leisure	Personal	Total
Aged <40, no kids	28 **	−32 **	−1	5	0
Kids 0–5	25 **	24 **	−46 **	−2	0
Kids 6–15	17 *	5	−21 **	−1	0
Older no kids (ref)					

(continued)

APPENDIX

Table I. *(continued)*

MEN	Paid	Unpaid	Leisure	Personal	Total
Full-time empl.	282 **	−62 **	−169 **	−52 **	0
Part-time empl.	129 *	−33 **	−88 **	−8	0
Non/unemployed (ref)					
Canada	14	12 *	−15	−11 *	0
Denmark	35 **	−55 **	57 **	−37 **	0
Netherlands	3	−15 **	13	−1	0
UK	24 *	−18 **	−33 **	26 **	0
USA	57 **	11 *	−67 **	−1	0
Finland (ref)					
1961–1971 (ref)					
1972–1981	−21 *	20 **	−1	3	0
1982–1995	−24 **	42 **	−15 *	−3	0
(Constant)	101	154 **	608 **	577 **	1440
Adj R Square	17	11	.14	.06	

** significant at .005   * significant at .05

Table II. Minutes Per Day in Four Unpaid Work Time-Use Categories: OLS Regression Coefficients for Women and Men

WOMEN	Core domestic	Child care	Shopping, etc.	Odd jobs	Total
Aged <40, no kids	−56 **	2	−1	−8 **	−64
Kids 0–5	15 **	94 **	3	−9 **	104
Kids 6–15	21 **	21 **	5 *	−5 *	42
Older no kids (ref)					
Full-time empl.	−101 **	−16 **	−15 **	−8 **	−140
Part-time empl.	−50 **	−12 **	−6 *	−4	−72
Non/unemployed (ref)					
Canada	−31 **	15 **	15 **	−5 *	−5
Denmark	−3	−25 **	−19 **	−11 **	−58
Netherlands	−9	3	7 *	4	5
UK	−1	−5	3	−0	−3
USA	−10*	10 **	24 **	6 *	29
Finland (ref)					
1961–1971 (ref)					
1972–1981	−46 **	2	3	4 *	−37
1982–1995	−61 **	11 **	6 *	10 **	−34
(Constant)	277 **	10 **	47	27	361
Adj R Square	.29	.35	.06	.03	

MEN	Core domestic	Child care	Shopping, etc.	Odd jobs	Total
Aged <40, no kids	−13 **	−1	−2	−16 **	−32
Kids 0–5	−4 *	31 **	2	−5	24
Kids 6–15	−6 **	7 **	2	2	5
Older no kids (ref)					
Full time empl.	−28 **	−4 **	−17 **	−13 **	−62
Part-time empl.	−16 **	−4	−6	−7	−33
Non/unemployed (ref)					
Canada	4	6 **	13 **	−11 **	12
Denmark	−3	−4 *	−20 **	−29 **	−55
Netherlands	−5	4 **	−6 *	−8 *	−15
UK	−6 *	−1	−13 **	2	−18
USA	3	3 *	16 **	−10 **	11
Finland (ref)					
1961–1971 (ref)					
1972–1981	8 **	4 **	2	6 *	20
1982–1995	18 **	7 **	4 *	14 **	42
(Constant)	52 **	−0	47 **	55 **	154
Adj R Square	.06	.16	.06	.04	

** significant at .005   * significant at .05

(These tables were originally published in Sullivan and Gershuny 2001.)

117

REFERENCES

Acock, A. C., and D. H. Demo
   1994   *Family Diversity and Well-Being*. Thousand Oaks, Calif.: Sage.
Adam, B.
   1995   *Timewatch: The Social Analysis of Time*. Cambridge, UK: Polity.
Alcoff, L.
   1988   Cultural feminism vs. poststructuralism. *Signs* 13 (3): 405–436.
Austin, J. L.
   1962   *How to Do Things with Words*. Oxford, UK: Oxford University Press.
Bailey, M. E.
   1993   Foucauldian feminism: Contesting bodies, sexuality and identity. In *Up Against Foucault*, ed. C. Ramazanoglu. New York: Routledge.
Barrett, M.
   1997   Capitalism and women's liberation. Reprinted in *The Second Wave: A Reader in Feminist Theory*, ed. L. Nicholson. New York: Routledge.
Bauman, Z.
   1987   *Legislators and Interpreters: On Modernity, Postmodernity and Intellectuals*. Cambridge, UK: Polity.
Baxter, J.
   1992   Power, attitudes and time: The domestic division of labor. *Journal of Comparative Family Studies* 23 (2): 165–182.
Baxter, J.
   1993   *Work at Home: The Domestic Division of Labor*. Queensland, Australia: University of Queensland Press.

REFERENCES

Beck, U., and E. Beck-Gernsheim
1995   *The Normal Chaos of Love*. Cambridge, UK: Polity.

Beck, U., A. Giddens, and S. Lasch
1994   *Reflexive Modernization*. Cambridge, UK: Polity.

Bellah, R. N., R. Madsen, W. M. Sullivan, A. Swidler, and S. M. Tipton
1985   *Habits of the Heart: Individualism and Commitment in American Life.* Berkeley: University of California Press.

Benjamin, O.
1995   *Self-Development and the Negotiability of Family Work.* Unpublished PhD thesis, University of Oxford.

Benjamin, O.
1998   Therapeutic discourse, power and change: Emotion and negotiation in marital conversations. *Sociology* 32 (4): 771–793.

Benjamin, O., and O. Sullivan
1996   The importance of difference: Conceptualising increased flexibility in gender relations at home. *Sociological Review* 44 (2): 225–251.

Benjamin, O., and O. Sullivan
1999   Relational resources, gender consciousness and possibilities of change in marital relationships. *Sociological Review* 47 (4): 794–820.

Berk, S. F.
1985   *The Gender Factory: The Apportionment of Work in American Households*. New York: Plenum.

Berkovitch, N.
1999   *From Motherhood to Citizenship: Women's Rights and International Organizations*. Baltimore: Johns Hopkins University Press.

Bianchi, S.
2000   Maternal employment and time with children: Dramatic change or surprising continuity? *Demography* 37 (4): 401–414.

Bielby, D., and W. T. Bielby
1988   She works hard for the money: Household responsibilities and the allocation of work effort. *American Journal of Sociology* 93 (5): 1031–1059.

Bittman, M.
1998   The land of the lost long weekend ? Trends in free time among working age Australians 1974–1992. *Loisir et société* 21 (2): 353–378.

Bittman, M., and F. Lovejoy
1993   Domestic power: Negotiating an unequal division of labour within a framework of equality. *Australian and New Zealand Journal of Sociology* 29 (3): 302–321.

Bittman, M., and J. Wajcman
2000   The rush hour: The character of leisure time and gender equity. *Social Forces* 79 (1): 165–189.

Blair-Loy, M.
2001   Cultural constructions of family schemas: The case of women finance executives. *Gender and Society* 15 (5): 687–709.

Blair-Loy, M., and J. A. Jacobs
2003   Globalization, work hours and the care deficit among stockbrokers. *Gender and Society* 17 (2): 230–249.

Bourdieu, P.
1984   *Distinction: A Social Critique of the Judgement of Taste.* London: Routledge & Kegan Paul.

Braidotti, R.
1991   *Patterns of Dissonance: A Study of Women in Contemporary Philosophy.* Cambridge, UK: Polity.

Brines, J.
1994   Economic dependency, gender and the division of labor at home. *American Journal of Sociology* 100 (3): 652–688.

Bucholtz, M.
1996   Black feminist theory and African American women's linguistic practice. In *Rethinking Language and Gender Research*, ed. V. L. Bergvall, J. M. Bing, and A. F. Freed. New York: Longman.

Bucholtz, M.
1999   Bad examples: Transgression and progress in language and gender studies. In *Reinventing Identities: The Gendered Self in Discourse*, ed. M. Bucholtz, A. C. Liang, and L. A. Sutton. Studies in Gender and Language. Oxford, UK: Oxford University Press.

Bucholtz, M., and K. Hall
2004   Theorizing identity in language and sexuality research. *Language in Society* 33: 469–515.

REFERENCES

Bucholtz, M., A. C. Liang, and L. A. Sutton, eds.
1999   *Reinventing Identities: The Gendered Self in Discourse.* Studies in Gender and Language. Oxford, UK: Oxford University Press.

Burgess, A.
1998   *Fatherhood Reclaimed.* London: Vermillion.

Cancian, F. M.
1987   *Love in America: Gender and Self-Development.* New York: Cambridge University Press.

Cancian, F. M., and S. L. Gordon
1988   Changing emotion norms in marriage: Love and anger in women's U.S. magazines since 1900. *Gender and Society* 2: 308–342.

Caplan, P., ed.
1987.   *The Cultural Construction of Sexuality.* London: Tavistock.

Cherlin, A.
1978   Remarriage as an incomplete institution. *American Journal of Sociology* 84: 634–650.

Clark, H. H.
1996   Communities, commonalities and communication. *In Rethinking Linguistic Relativity*, ed. J. J. Gumperz and S. C. Levinson. Cambridge, UK: Cambridge University Press.

Coates, J.
1986   *Women, Men and Language.* London: Longman.

Coltrane, S.
1989   Household labor and the routine production of gender. *Social Problems* 36: 473–490.

Coltrane, S.
1996   *Family Man: Fatherhood, Housework and Gender Equity.* Oxford, UK: Oxford University Press.

Coltrane, S.
1998   *Gender and Families.* Thousand Oaks, Calif.: Pine Forge.

Coltrane, S.
2000   Research on household labor: Modeling and measuring the social embeddedness of routine family work. *Journal of Marriage and the Family* 62 (4): 1208–1233.

Connell, R. W.
1987   *Gender and Power.* Cambridge, UK: Polity.

Connell, R. W.
2000   *The Men and the Boys.* Cambridge, UK: Polity.

Connell, R. W.
2002   *Gender: Short Introductions.* Malden, Mass.: Blackwell.

Crawford, M.
1995   *Talking Difference: On Gender and Language.* London: Sage.

Crompton, R.
1996   Paid employment and the changing system of gender relations. *Sociology* 30 (3): 427–445.

Crompton, R., ed.
1999   *Restructuring Gender Relations and Employment.* Oxford, UK: Oxford University Press.

Crompton, R., and F. Harris
1999   Attitudes, women's employment and the changing domestic division of labor. In *Restructuring Gender Relations and Employment*, ed. R. Crompton. Oxford, UK: Oxford University Press.

Crouch, C., and W. Streeck, eds.
1997   *Political Economy of Modern Capitalism.* London: Sage.

Curzan, A.
2003   *Gender Shifts in the History of English.* Cambridge: Cambridge University Press.

Dancer, L. S., and L. A. Gilbert
1993   Spouses' family work participation and its relation to wives' occupational level. *Sex Roles* 28: 127–145.

Demo, D. H., and A. C. Acock
1993   Family diversity and the division of domestic labor: How much have things really changed? *Family Relations* 42: 323–331.

Dench, G., ed.
1999   *Rewriting the Sexual Contract.* New Brunswick, N.J.: Transaction.

Deutsch, F. M.
1999   *Halving It All.* Boston: Harvard University Press.

REFERENCES

DeVault, M. L.
1991 *Feeding the Family: The Social Organization of Caring as Gendered Work.* Chicago: University of Chicago Press.

Dex, S.
1988 *Women's Attitudes to Work.* London: Macmillan.

Doucet, A.
1992 What difference does difference make: Towards an understanding of gender equality and difference in the household division of labor. In *Inequalities in Employment, Inequalities in Home Life*, ed. G. Dunne, R. M. Blackburn, and J. Jarman. Cambridge, UK: Cambridge University Press.

Doucet, A.
1996 Encouraging voices: Towards more creative methods for collecting data on gender and household labor. In *Gender Relations in Public and Private*, ed. L. Morris and E. S. Lyon. London: Macmillan.

Dow, G. K., and F. T. Juster
1985 Goods, time and well-being: The joint dependence problem. In *Time, Goods, and Well-Being*, ed. F. T. Juster and F. P. Stafford. Ann Arbor: Survey Research Centre, University of Michigan.

Duncombe, J., and D. Marsden
1993 Love and intimacy: The gender division of emotion and "emotion work." *Sociology* 27 (2): 221–241.

Eckert, P., and S. McConnell-Ginet
2003 *Language and Gender.* Cambridge, UK: Cambridge University Press.

Edgell, S.
1980 *Middle Class Couples.* London: Allen & Unwin.

Eisenstadt, S. N.
1978 *Revolution and the Transformation of Societies: A Comparative Study of Civilizations.* New York: Free Press.

Fraser, N.
1997 Structuralism or pragmatics? In *The Second Wave: A Reader in Feminist Theory*, ed. L. Nicholson. London: Routledge.

Gershuny, J.
1990 International comparisons of time budget surveys: Methods and opportunities. In *Zeitbudgeterhebungen*, ed. R. von Schweitzer, M. Ehling, and D. Schafer. Stuttgart, Germany: Metzler-Poeschel.

Gershuny, J.
1995   Time budget research in Europe. *Statistics in Transition* 2 (4): 1–23.

Gershuny, J.
2000   *Changing Times: Work and Leisure in Postindustrial Society.* Oxford, UK: Oxford University Press.

Gershuny J., M. Godwin, and S. Jones
1994   The domestic labour revolution: A process of lagged adaptation? In *The Social and Political Economy of the Household,* ed. M. Anderson, F. Bechoffer, and J. I. Gershuny. Oxford, UK: Oxford University Press.

Gershuny, J., and S. Jones
1987   The changing work-leisure balance in Britain 1961–1984. *Sociological Review* 33: 9–50.

Gershuny, J., and O. Sullivan
1998   Sociological uses of time-use diary data. *European Sociological Review* 14 (1): 69–85.

Gerson, K.
1993   *No Man's Land: Men's Changing Commitments to Work and Family Life.* New York: Basic.

Gerson, K.
2001   Dilemmas of involved fatherhood. In *Shifting the Center: Understanding Contemporary Families,* ed. S. J. Ferguson. Mountain View, Calif.: Mayfield.

Gerson, J. M., and K. Peiss
1985   Boundaries, negotiation, consciousness: Reconceptualizing gender relations. *Social Problems* 32: 317–331.

Giddens, A.
1984   *The Constitution of Society.* Cambridge, UK: Polity.

Giddens, A.
1990   *The Consequences of Modernity.* Cambridge, UK: Polity.

Giddens, A.
1991   *Modernity and Self Identity.* Cambridge, UK: Polity.

Giddens, A.
1992   *The Transformation of Intimacy.* Cambridge, UK: Polity.

REFERENCES

Goldscheider, F. K., and L. J. Waite
1991 *New Families, No Families: The Transformation of the American Home.* Berkeley: University of California Press.

Goodnew, J., and J. Bowes
1994 *Men, Women and Household Work.* Melbourne: Oxford University Press.

Gupta, S.
1999 The effects of marital status transitions on men's housework performance. *Journal of Marriage and the Family* 61: 700–711.

Hall, K., and M. Bucholtz
1995 *Gender Articulated: Language and the Socially Constructed Self.* New York: Routledge.

Hearn, J.
1999 A crisis for masculinity, or new agendas for men? In *New Agendas for Women*, ed. S. Walby. London: Macmillan.

Heath, J. A., and W. D. Bourne
1995 Husbands and housework: Parity or parody? *Social Science Quarterly* 76: 195–202.

Hewlett, S. A.
1991 *When the Bough Breaks.* New York: Basic.

Hochschild, A. R.
1979 Emotion work, feeling rules, and social structure. *American Journal of Sociology* 85: 551–575.

Hochschild, A. R.
1989 *The Second Shift: Working Parents and the Revolution at Home.* Berkeley: University of California Press.

Hochschild, A. R.
1994 The commercial spirit of intimate life and the abduction of feminism: Signs from women's advice books. *Theory, Culture and Society* 11: 1–24.

Hochschild, A. R.
1995 Understanding the future of fatherhood. In *Changing Fatherhood: An Interdisciplinary Perspective*, ed. M. C. P. van Dougen, G. Frinking, and M. Jacobs. Amsterdam: Thesis Publishers.

Hochschild, A. R.
1997 *The Time Bind.* New York: Henry Holt.

Hofstede, G., ed.

1998   *Masculinity and Femininity: The Taboo Dimension of National Cultures.* Cross-Cultural Psychology Series. Thousand Oaks, Calif.: Sage.

Hood, J. C., ed.

1993   *Men, Work and Family.* Newbury Park, Calif.: Sage.

Illouz, E.

1991   Reason within passion: Love in women's magazines. *Critical Studies in Mass Communication* 8: 231–248.

Inglehart, R.

1997   *Modernization and Postmodernization: Cultural, Economic and Political Change in 43 Societies.* New York: Princeton University Press.

Ishii-Kuntz, M., and S. Coltrane

1992   Remarriage, stepparenting and household labor. *Journal of Family Issues* 13 (2): 215–233.

Jacobs, J. A., and K. Gerson

1998   Who are the overworked Americans? *Review of Social Economy* 1 (4): 442–459.

Jamieson, L.

1998   *Intimacy.* Cambridge, UK: Polity.

Jamieson, L.

1999   Intimacy transformed? A critical look at the "pure relationship." *Sociology* 33 (3): 477–494.

Juster, F. T.

1985   The validity and quality of time use estimates obtained from recall diaries. In *Time, Goods, and Well-Being,* ed. F. T. Juster and F. P. Stafford. Ann Arbor: Survey Research Centre, University of Michigan.

Kalfs, N.

1993   *Hour by Hour: Effects of the Data Collection Mode in Time Use Research.* Amsterdam: Nederlands Instituut voor Maatschappij en Markt-Onderzoek.

Kitzinger, C.

1998   "Emotion work" as a participant resource: A feminist analysis of young women's talk-in-interaction. *Sociology* 32 (2): 299–320.

REFERENCES

Kitzinger, C.
  2001   "Snatch," "Hole" or "Honey-pot"? Semantic categories and the prob-
         lem of nonspecificity in female genital slang. *Journal of Sex Research*
         38 (2): 146–158.

Kluwer, E. S., J. M. Heesink, and E. Van de Vliert
  1996   Marital conflict about the division of household labor and paid work.
         Journal of Marriage and the Family 58: 958–969.

Knijn, T.
  1995   Towards post-paternalism? In *Changing Fatherhood: An Interdiscipli-
         nary Perspective*, ed. M. C. P. van Dougen, G. Frinking, and M. Ja-
         cobs, M. Amsterdam: Thesis Publishers.

Komter, A.
  1989   Hidden power in marriage. *Gender and Society* 3 (2): 187–216.

Lakoff, R.
  1975   *Language and Women's Place*. New York: Harper & Row.

Lamb, M. E., ed.
  1986   *The Father's Role: Applied Perspectives*. London: John Wiley.

Le Goff, J.
  1981   Temps et société chrétienne au moyen âge. *Temps libre* 3: 111–116.

Lennon, M. C., and S. Rosenfield
  1994   Relative fairness and the division of housework: The importance of
         options. *American Journal of Sociology* 100 (2): 506–531.

Lewis, R. A.
  1986   Men's changing roles in marriage and the family. In *Men's Changing
         Roles in the Family*, ed. R. A. Lewis and M. B. Sussman. New York:
         Haworth.

Lewis, R. A., and M. B. Sussman, eds.
  1986   *Men's Changing Roles in the Family*. New York: Haworth.

Lorber, J.
  1987   Editor's introduction to C. West and D. H. Zimmerman, Doing gen-
         der. *Gender and Society* 1: 125–151.

Lorber, J.
  1994   *Paradoxes of Gender*. New Haven, Conn.: Yale University Press.

Losh-Hesselbart, S.
1988   Cohort and gender attitude change: Further shifts in public opinion. Paper presented at the American Sociological Association annual conference, Atlanta.

Lupri, E., ed.
1983   *The Changing Position of Women in Family Society*. Leiden, Netherlands: E. J. Brill.

Market Research Society
1991   *Occupational Grading: A Job Dictionary*. 4th ed. London: Market Research Society.

Marx Ferree, M.
1990   Beyond separate spheres: Feminism and family research. *Journal of Marriage and the Family* 52: 866–884.

Marx Ferree, M.
1991   The gender division of labour in two-earner marriages: Dimensions of variability and change. *Journal of Family Issues* 12: 158–180.

McMahon, A.
1999   *Taking Care of Men: Sexual Politics in the Public Mind*. Cambridge, UK: Cambridge University Press.

Morgan, D. H. J.
1985   *The Family, Politics and Social Theory*. London: Routledge & Kegan Paul.

Morgan, D. H. J.
1996   *Family Connections: An Introduction to Family Studies*. Cambridge, UK: Polity.

Morris, L.
1990   *The Workings of the Household*. Cambridge, UK: Polity.

Morris, L. and E. S. Lyon, eds.
1996   *Gender Relations in Public and Private*. London: Macmillan.

Nilsen, A. P
1987   Guidelines against sexist language: A case history. In *Women and Language in Transition*, ed. J. Penfeld. New York: State University of New York Press.

REFERENCES

Niemi, I.
  1995   A general view of time use by gender. In *Time Use of Women in Europe and North America*, ed. I. Niemi. New York: United Nations Economic Commission for Europe.

Oakley, A.
  1974   *The Sociology of Housework*. London: Martin Robinson.

Orbuch, T. L., and S. L. Eyster
  1997   Division of household labor among Black couples and White couples. *Social Forces* 76: 301–332.

Pahl, J.
  1989   *Money and Marriage*. London: Macmillan.

Penfeld, J., ed.
  1987   *Women and Language in Transition*. New York: State University of New York Press.

Pesquera, B.
  1997   In the beginning he wouldn't even lift a spoon. In *Situated Lives: Gender and Culture in Everyday Life*, ed. L. Lamphere, H. Ragone, and P. Zavella. London: Routledge.

Pleck, J. H.
  1985   *Working Wives/Working Husbands*. Beverly Hills, Calif.: Sage.

Pleck, J. H.
  1993   Are family-supportive employer policies relevant to men? In *Men, Work and Family*, ed. J. C. Hood. Newbury Park, Calif.: Sage.

Pleck, J. H., M. E. Lamb, and J. A. Levine
  1986   Epilog: Facilitating future change in men's family roles. In *Men's Changing Roles in the Family*, ed. R. A. Lewis and M. B. Sussman. New York: Haworth.

Plummer, K.
  1995   *Telling Sexual Stories: Power, Change and Social Worlds*. London: Routledge.

Pyke, K.
  1994   Women's employment as gift or burden? Marital power across marriage, divorce and remarriage. *Gender and Society* 8 (1): 73–91.

Pyke, K., and S. Coltrane
1996   Entitlement, obligation and gratitude in family work. *Journal of Family Issues* 17 (1): 60–82.

Risman, B.
1998   *Gender Vertigo.* New Haven, Conn.: Yale University Press.

Risman, B.
2004   Gender as social structure: Theory wrestling with activism. *Gender and Society* 18 (4): 429–450.

Robinson, J. P.
1985   The validity and reliability of diaries versus alternative time use measures. In *Time, Goods, and Well-Being,* ed. F. T. Juster and F. P. Stafford. Ann Arbor: Survey Research Centre, University of Michigan.

Robinson, J. P., and P. E. Converse
1972   Social change reflected in the use of time. In *The Human Meaning of Social Change,* ed. A. V. Campbell and P. E. Converse. New York: Russell Sage.

Robinson, J. P., and G. Godbey
1997   *Time for Life: The Surprising Ways Americans Use Their Time.* University Park, Pa.: Penn State University Press.

Sanchez, L.
1993   Women's power and the gendered division of domestic labor in the third world. *Gender and Society* 7: 434–459.

Sanchez, L., and E. Kane
1996   Women's and men's constructions of perceptions of housework fairness *Journal of Family Issues* 17: 358–387.

Saville, J.
1975   The welfare state: An historical process. In *Social Welfare in Modern Britain,* ed. E. Butterworth and R. Holman. London: Fontana.

Schwartz, P.
1994   *Peer Marriage: How Love between Equals Really Works.* New York: Free Press.

Schwartz, P.
2001   Peer Marriage. In *Shifting the Center: Understanding Contemporary Families,* ed. S. J. Ferguson. Mountain View, Calif.: Mayfield.

REFERENCES

Scott, J.
1999   Family change: Revolution or backlash in attitudes? In *Changing Britain: Families and Households in the 1990s*, ed. S. McRae. Oxford, UK: Oxford University Press.

Scott, J., D. F. Alwin, and M. Brown
1996   Changing sex-role attitudes. *Sociology* 30 (3): 427–445.

Searle, J.
1969   *Speech Acts*. Cambridge, UK: Cambridge University Press.

Segal, L.
1990   *Slow Motion: Changing Masculinities, Changing Men*. London: Virago.

Shaw, J.
1998   "Feeling a list coming on": Gender and the pace of life. *Time and Society* 7 (2): 383–396.

Shelton, B. A.
1992   *Women, Men and Time: Gender Differences in Paid Work, Housework and Leisure*. (Contributions in Women's Studies 127). New York: Greenwood.

Shelton, B. A., and D. John
1993   Ethnicity, race and difference: A comparison of White, Black and Hispanic men's household labor time. In *Men, Work and Family*, ed. J. C. Hood. Newbury Park, Calif.: Sage.

Simonds, W.
1992   *Women and Self-Help Culture: Reading between the Lines*. New Brunswick, N.J.: Rutgers University Press.

Skolnick, A.
1992   *The Intimate Environment: Exploring Marriage and the Family*. 5th ed. New York: HarperCollins.

Smart, C., and B. Neale
1999   *Family Fragments?* Cambridge, UK: Polity.

Smitherman, G.
1977   *Talkin and Testifyin*. Boston: Houghton Mifflin.

Southerton, D., E. Shove, and A. Warde
2001   "Harried and hurried": Time shortage and the co-ordination of everyday life. *CRIC Discussion Paper 47*: University of Manchester & UMIST.

Spender, D.
1980   *Man Made Language.* London: Pandora.

Spitze, G.
1986   The division of task responsibility in U.S. households: Longitudinal adjustments to change. *Social Forces* 64 (3): 689–701.

Stones, R.
1996   *Sociological Reasoning: Towards a Past-Modern Sociology.* London: Macmillan.

Sullivan, O.
1997a   The division of household work among "remarried" couples. *Journal of Family Issues* 18 (2): 205–223.

Sullivan, O.
1997b   Time waits for no (wo)man: An investigation of the gendered experience of domestic time. *Sociology* 31 (2): 221–239.

Sullivan, O.
2000   The division of domestic labor: 20 years of change? *Sociology* 34 (3): 437–456.

Sullivan, O.
2004   Changing gender practices within the household: A theoretical perspective. *Gender and Society* 18 (2): 207–223.

Sullivan, O., and J. Gershuny
2001   Cross-national changes in time-use: Some sociological (hi)stories re-examined. *British Journal of Sociology* 52 (2): 331–347.

Swidler, A.
1985   Love and marriage. In *Habits of the Heart,* ed. R. N. Bellah, R. Madsen, W. M. Sullivan, A. Swidler, and S. M. Tipton. Berkeley: University of California Press.

Thompson, E. P.
1965   Time, work-discipline and industrial capitalism. *Past and Present* 38: 56–97.

Thompson, L.
1991   Family work: Women's sense of fairness. *Journal of Family Issues* 12 (2): 181–196.

Thompson, L.
1993   Conceptualising gender in marriage: The case of marital care. *Journal of Marriage and the Family* 55: 557–569.

REFERENCES

Thornton, A.
1989   Changing attitudes towards family issues in the United States. *Journal of Marriage and the Family* 51: 873–93.

Van Den Bergh, N.
1987   Renaming: Vehicle for empowerment. In *Women and Language in Transition*, ed. J. Penfeld. New York: State University of New York Press.

Vanek, J.
1974   Time spent in housework. *Scientific American* 231: 116–120.

Veblen, T.
1967   *The Theory of the Leisure Class*. New York: Viking.

Vogler, C.
1994   Money in the household. In *The Social and Political Economy of the Household*, ed. M. Anderson, F. Bechhofer, and J. Gershuny. Oxford, UK: Oxford University Press.

Voydanoff, P., and B. W. Donnelly
1999   The intersection of time in activities and perceived unfairness in relation to psychological distress and marital quality. *Journal of Marriage and the Family* 61: 739–751

Walby, S.
1997   *Gender Transformations*. London: Routledge.

Warde, A., and K. Hetherington
1993   A changing domestic division of labour? Issues of measurement and interpretation. *Work, Employment and Society* 7 (1): 23–45.

Weeks, J., B. Heaphy, and C. Donovan
1999   Families of choice: Autonomy and mutuality in non-heterosexual relationships. In *Changing Britian: Families and Households in the 1990s*, ed. S. McRae. Oxford, UK: Oxford University Press.

West, C., and S. Fenstermaker
1993   Power, inequality and the accomplishment of gender: An ethnomethodological view. In *Theory on Gender/Feminism on Theory*, ed. P. England. New York: Aldine de Gruyter.

West, C., and D. H. Zimmerman
1987   Doing gender. *Gender and Society* 1: 125–151.

Wheelock, J.
1990 *Husbands at Home: The Domestic Economy in a Postindustrial Society.*
London: Routledge.

Willinger, B.
1993 Resistance and change. In *Men, Work and Family*, ed. J. C. Hood.
London: Sage.

Young, M., and P. Willmott
1973 *The Symmetrical Family.* London: Routledge & Kegan Paul.

Zalewski, M.
2000 *Feminism after Postmodernism.* London: Routledge.

Zvonkovic, A., K. Greaves, C. Schmiege, and L. Hall
1996 The marital construction of gender through work and family deci-
sions: A qualitative analysis. *Journal of Marriage and the Family* 58:
91–100.

INDEX

) (

ABOUT THE AUTHOR

) (

Oriel Sullivan teaches sociology in the Department of Behavioral Sciences, Ben Gurion University, Israel, having worked previously for many years in the Department of Sociology at the University of Essex, England. Her main areas of research are families and households, with a focus on the domestic division of labor as a key arena of potential transformation in gender relations. She has written extensively on the use of time-use diary data to investigate aspects of the domestic division of labor and the use of time more generally among couples. Professor Sullivan does much of her creative thinking while walking her dogs in the southern Negev desert, on the cliffs above the African Rift Valley.